Preaching Jesus

Christ-Centered Gospel Preaching

Christopher Findley, MDiv

Preaching Jesus

Version 1

Copyright © 2025 by AdventPreaching.com

All rights reserved. No part of this book may be reproduced or transmitted in any form or by any means without written permission from the author.

ISBN: 9798304076869

Printed in the USA
ChristopherFindley – Christopher@AdventPreaching.com
Youtube.com/AdventPreaching
Follow @PreachingJesusEverywhere
@AdventPreaching (Instagram)

Scriptures references other than from the King James Version quoted by permission in this workbook are as follows:

ESV. Bible text credited to ESV are from The Holy Bible, English Standard Version® (ESV©)

NIV. Bible text credited to NIV are from The Holy Bible, NEW INTERNATIONAL VERSION®, Copyright © 1973, 1978,1984, 2011 by Biblica, Inc. ® Used by permission. All rights reserved worldwide.

NKJV. Bible text credited to NKJV are from the New King James Version ®. Copyright © 1982 by Thomas Nelson. Used By permission. All rights reserved.

Acknowledgements

I would like to begin by honoring the great preachers who came before me—men and women whose faithfulness in proclaiming the Gospel has inspired me to preach Jesus and walk closely with Him. I am especially grateful to Dr. Bill Kilgore at Southwestern Adventist University and Dr. Hyveth Williams. Their Christ-centered preaching, wisdom, and example have profoundly shaped my ministry and deepened my commitment to sharing the transformational power of the Word.

I also want to express my heartfelt gratitude to my students at Burton Academy. Your sermons, questions, and passion for the Bible have inspired me more than you know. Listening to your preaching revealed a deep need for accessible resources on Christ-centered biblical preaching—tools that will equip and empower the next generation to boldly proclaim the Gospel.

To the teachers, pastors, and parents who have discipled me over the years, thank you for nurturing my faith and helping me grow in Christ. I have been blessed beyond measure by your influence, encouragement, and love. A special thanks to my wife, Karen—my closest discipler and constant source of strength. Karen, your prayers, thoughtful insights, and loving challenges continue to shape me daily. Thank you for creating a home where faith is not just practiced but lived in every moment.

Finally, I give all glory, honor, and praise to the ultimate Preacher—Jesus Christ. Through His life, example, and the power of the Holy Spirit, He calls us to be His disciples and to disciple others. May this work serve His purpose and bring glory to His name in every season. Amen.

Contents

1: Calling: Christ-Centered Biblical Preaching — 9

2: Prayer: Holy Spirit Our True Source — 23

3: Character: Loving Jesus before we Preach Him — 31

4. Bible Study: Face to Face with Jesus

5. Outline: 7 Steps for Christ-centered Sermons — 61

4: Problem: Jesus Victory in the Great Controversy — 68

5: Solution: Jesus the Solution to Every Situation — 76

6: Gospel: Preach the Gospel in Every Message — 85

7: Application: for Transformation in Jesus — 97

8: Appeal: Calling for Life Transformation — 105

9: Crafting an Introduction: Grabbing Attention — 111

9: Learning: Growing in Preaching Christ — 11

Appendix 25+ Christ-Centered Sermons — 130

Bibliography — 222

Preface

Importance of Christ-Centered Biblical Preaching

The Need for Christ-Centered Preaching

The purpose of this study is to emphasize the urgent need for Christ-centered Biblical sermons in our pulpits today. It is the Gospel that transforms hearts. As one of my favorite Christian writers states, "Put Christ into every sermon. Let the preciousness, mercy, and glory of Jesus Christ be dwelt upon until Christ is formed within, the hope of glory" (RH, March 19, 1895).

Christ as the Center of Preaching

In John 12:32, Jesus says, "And I, if I be lifted up from the earth, will draw all men unto me." The focus of every sermon should be Christ. Ellen White affirms this, saying, "These are our themes—Christ crucified for our sins, Christ risen from the dead, Christ our intercessor before God..." (Evangelism, p. 187). As we proclaim the Gospel, it is crucial that we present Christ's sacrifice as the central theme, for it is the cross that draws souls to Him.

The Gospel and Its Power

In my journey of understanding the hope and healing found in the Gospel, I have encountered many sermons that, while Biblically sound, miss the essential Gospel connection. Preaching without Christ is like a meal without flavor. "Lift Him up, the Saviour of souls," Ellen White encourages, "lift Him up higher and still higher..." (Evangelism, p. 187). The Gospel must be presented in every sermon as the message of salvation through Jesus Christ.

Preaching Christ in Every Message

Every sermon should tell the story of Jesus—His life, self-denial, sacrifice, death, resurrection, and intercession for us (VSS 312). It is in lifting up Jesus that hearts are transformed and souls are drawn to the Gospel. The cross, as Ellen White writes, "explains all other mysteries" (*The Great Controversy*, p. 652).

The central theme of every sermon must be the redemptive work of Christ. Through His death, resurrection, and intercession, the Gospel is proclaimed, offering healing and peace to all who hear. Our task is to point the listeners to Jesus, for "Behold the Lamb of God, which taketh away the sin of the world" (John 1:29).

Conclusion: Christ-Centered Preaching

The challenge of preaching is to focus on Christ as the center of all Scripture. As we proclaim the Word of God, we must do so in the light of the cross, remembering that every truth in the Bible is illuminated by the sacrifice of Christ (Evangelism, p. 190). Our mission is clear: to lift up Jesus, proclaim His salvation, and trust that, as He promised, "I, if I be lifted up from the earth, will draw all men unto me" (John 12:32).

1

The Great Need: Gospel Filled Christ-Centered Biblical Sermons

"Preach and live as if Jesus was crucified yesterday, rose from the dead today, and is returning tomorrow."
— *Martin Luther*

That was a Gospel-filled Christ-Centered Biblical[1] Sermon! That is one that that I pray to say after a preacher sits down. Unfortunately I have come to the seminary and I was very excited to hear all the preaching from the top expositors in the world but I have not always had that response. When I brought it up to a preaching professor that Christ was not mentioned in the sermon or connected to the main point. It was as if I committed a crime or was disrespectful for pointing

---

[1] Jesus is the incarnate Word (John 1:14); faithful preaching must convey this truth, allowing congregants to encounter Christ through Scripture.Karoline M. Lewis, *A Lay Preacher's Guide* (Minneapolis: Fortress Press, 2020), 1.

it out. Preaching Jesus has been a burden on my heart ever since I come to a realization that my works cannot save me its only by looking to what Jesus has already done for me and allowing the Holy Spirit to guide and empower me am I able to walk righteously with God. This is the Good News of the Gospel that it is not based on my personal strength but by abiding in Jesus is my victory.

    There is a lack of Gospel-filled Christ-centered Biblical Preaching in our pulpits. Yes we are called to preach Scripture[2]. Yes we are called to break down the Hebrew and Greek. Yes we are called to preach against Sin. All those things are correct. But every Christian sermon requirement is to Preach JESUS. To uplift the life, death and resurrection of Jesus Christ. John 12:32 - " And I, when I am lifted up from the earth, will draw all people to myself." Every Christian sermon must be Gospel focused, Holy Spirit filled, Redemptive based with the main points of the sermon pointing us to our Lord and Saviour Jesus Christ. Why? Because Jesus is the only name that can save! Acts 4:12 ESV - And there is salvation in no one else, for there is no other name under heaven given among men by which we must be saved." So when we go to prepare a sermon one of our prayers to God is to have a personal encounter of transformation with Jesus in the text. To meet Jesus our living reality face to face in the text and to study the text with Jesus. John 5:39 - "Search the Scriptures, for in them ye think ye have eternal life; and it is they which testify of Me.

---

[2] Jesus is the "Word of God" (John 1:1), making biblical preaching a **living encounter with Him**. Lewis, *A Lay Preacher's Guide*, 6.

Some will argue back and say that we dont need to mention Jesus or the Good News of the Gospel in every sermon. The argument is that when we preach Scripture we are automatically preaching the good news and Jesus. Ofcourse I disagree because if that was the case then we could simply stand in the pulpit and read scripture or preach the exact words of scripture with passion. But the sermon is the place to Introduce the Biblical story, Transition to the problem/situation in the Bible and connect it to the overall theme of the Great Controversy then proceed to share the Biblical Solution and how that connects to Jesus. "Jesus—only Jesus—should be at the center of everything for anyone called to share the good news of the cross, the empty tomb, and His soon return. Preaching isn't just about mentioning Jesus; it's about making Him the heart and soul of every message. Like Paul said in 1 Corinthians 2:2, *'For I decided to know nothing among you except Jesus Christ and Him crucified.'*"[3]

After we point it to Jesus we break down the main point of the sermon and how that connects to the Good News of the Gospel. After we finish the first half of the sermon now its time to go to the second half of the sermon which is the application, Conclusion and the appeal. The application is the building of the bridge and how it connects to our lives. Where we connect the Biblical situation to our lives today and just like how God shows His grace throughout Scripture Jesus is seeking to pour His grace into our lives today. This is at the

---

[3] —Russell Burrill, *Adventist Evangelistic Preaching* (Hagerstown, MD: Review and Herald, 2012), 72.

center of every Holy Spirit filled sermon that God is seeking to pour out His grace and transform our lives. (Romans 12:2) The conclusion is a summary of the main points in one concise paragraph that transitions into the call for transformation in Jesus Christ in the appeal.

It is important to find balance in preaching between rebuking and encouraging listeners to walk with God and to repent of their sinful ways. It is just as important to encourage them that God is with them in their struggles and traumas of life seeking to heal them and pour out His love into their situations but most of all their hearts. Redemptive, Transforming, Empowering Grace.[4] Preaching is not just for us to hear a good sermon about God but to faithfully accept the living word into our lives and walk in a life of discipleship in Jesus Christ.[5]

Preaching the Gospel Includes :
1. Proclaiming the good news of salvation in Jesus Christ in a particular place and time[6]
2. Interpretation of the Gospel in connection to a Biblical Text that is relevant to shape their lives to grow in a personal faithful relationship with Jesus Christ

---

[4] 1. Gennifer Benjamin Brooks, *Good News Preaching: Offering the Gospel in Every Sermon* (Pilgrim Press, 2011).

[5] 1. Gennifer Benjamin Brooks, *Good News Preaching: Offering the Gospel in Every Sermon* (Pilgrim Press, 2011).

[6] 1. Gennifer Benjamin Brooks, *Good News Preaching: Offering the Gospel in Every Sermon* (Pilgrim Press, 2011). 2

Here's a practical list of things a preacher can do with the Scriptures they are working with to ensure their sermons are **Gospel-filled, Christ-centered, and transformational**:

1. Encounter Jesus in the Text

- **Prayerful Study:** Before preparing the sermon, pray to personally meet Jesus in the text. Ask the Holy Spirit to reveal Christ in a transformative way. When Christ comes face to face with you in the text that is the sermon. Where did you /Do we come face to face with Christ in the Text?
- **Ask Reflective Questions:**
    - Where is Jesus in this passage?
    - How does this text point to the life, death, resurrection, and intercession of Jesus?
    - How does this text reveal God's redemptive plan through Christ?
- **Search for Christ's Character:** Identify attributes of Christ (e.g., love, grace, justice) revealed in the passage.

Here is a list that you can reflect on when studying a Biblical Passage: (Feel free to Update)

Love – Christ's selfless, sacrificial, and unconditional love. (John 15:13; Romans 5:8)

Grace – His unmerited favor, forgiveness, and compassion toward sinners. (Ephesians 2:8-9; John 1:14)

Justice – His fairness, righteousness, and commitment to truth. (Isaiah 9:7; Revelation 19:11)

Mercy – His tender compassion and willingness to forgive. (Luke 6:36; Titus 3:5)

Holiness – His purity, sinlessness, and divine nature. (Hebrews 7:26; 1 Peter 1:15-16)

Humility – His willingness to serve, even unto death. (Philippians 2:5-8; Matthew 11:29)

Patience – His long-suffering and endurance with humanity. (2 Peter 3:9; 1 Timothy 1:16)

Faithfulness – His trustworthiness and unwavering commitment to God's will. (2 Thessalonians 3:3; Revelation 19:11)

Obedience – His complete submission to the Father's plan. (John 6:38; Hebrews 5:8)

Meekness – Strength under control, showing gentleness and peace. (Matthew 5:5; Matthew 21:5)

Wisdom – His divine insight, discernment, and teaching. (Colossians 2:3; Matthew 7:28-29)

Power – His authority over nature, sickness, death, and sin. (Matthew 28:18; Luke 8:24-25)

Truth – Christ as the embodiment of truth and integrity. (John 14:6; John 18:37)

Compassion – His empathy for the broken, needy, and lost. (Matthew 9:36; Mark 6:34)

Forgiveness – His readiness to forgive sins and restore relationships. (Luke 23:34; 1 John 1:9)

Righteousness – His moral perfection and alignment with God's standard. (1 John 2:1; 2 Corinthians 5:21)

Servanthood – His example of serving others humbly and wholeheartedly. (Mark 10:45; John 13:14-15)

Peace – His ability to bring peace to hearts, relationships, and situations. (John 14:27; Ephesians 2:14)

Joy – His deep, enduring joy rooted in His relationship with the Father. (John 15:11; Hebrews 12:2)

Sovereignty – His divine authority and control over all creation. (Colossians 1:16-17; Revelation 1:8)

Generosity – His willingness to give abundantly, including Himself. (2 Corinthians 8:9; John 10:10-11)

Boldness – His courage to speak truth and confront sin with love. (John 7:26; Matthew 23:13-39)

Gentleness – His tender approach to the weak and brokenhearted. (Matthew 12:20; Isaiah 40:11)

Perseverance – His unwavering determination to fulfill God's mission. (Hebrews 12:2-3; Luke 9:51)

Self-Control – His ability to restrain power and act according to the Father's will. (1 Peter 2:23; Matthew 26:53-54)

Christ Character Connection Writing Template

<u>Use this as a Template and Write This Down</u>

Today, we turn our hearts to a reflection of Christ: His _____ (insert characteristic, e.g., love, grace, justice). Our guide is _____ (insert Biblical reference, e.g., John 15:13), where His _____ (insert characteristic) is not just spoken but revealed—woven into _____ (describe the specific action, event, or teaching). Here, the character of Christ becomes a living portrait, showing us _____ (explain the theological or spiritual significance and how it reflects Christ's nature).

Think of _____ (insert a practical illustration, story, or personal reflection)—a glimpse of this truth in our own lives, like light breaking through clouds. What does this tell us? That Christ's _____ (insert characteristic) is not a distant ideal but a present invitation. It calls us to _____ (apply the lesson to the listener's life), to let this truth take root deep within us.

How should we respond? Perhaps with _____ (suggest practical steps: surrender, gratitude, sharing the Gospel), letting Christ's _____ (insert characteristic) shape our steps, soften our hearts, and fill our lives.

So, let us pause, let us lean in. Let us behold His _____ (insert characteristic) and let it transform us, not just for today but for eternity."

Christ- Connection Paragraph Template for

David & Goliath - 1 Samuel 17

"Today, we turn our hearts to a reflection of Christ: His **courage**. Our guide is **1 Samuel 17**, where courage is not just spoken but revealed—woven into the story of David and Goliath. Here, we see Christ's courage foreshadowed in David's boldness to stand against the giant. It is more than bravery; it is a trust-filled confidence that God fights the battles we cannot win alone.

Picture the scene: a young shepherd, armed not with weapons of war but with faith in the living God, faces an enemy no one else would dare confront. In David's courage, we glimpse the courage of Christ, who stood against sin, death, and the forces of darkness—not with sword and shield, but with the cross and His perfect sacrifice.

What does this tell us? That true courage comes not from our strength but from the presence of God within us. Like David, we are called to face the giants in our lives—fear, doubt, temptation—trusting that **the battle belongs to the Lord** (1 Samuel 17:47).

How should we respond? By laying down our fear and stepping forward with faith. By trusting in God's power, not our own. By letting Christ's courage live through us—speaking truth, loving boldly, and walking in His strength.

So, let us pause and reflect: what giants do we face today? Let us, like David, lean on the courage of Christ, who already overcame the greatest battle. And may His victory become ours, not just for today, but for eternity."**

2. Interpret the Text in a Christ-Centered Framework

- **Introduce the Biblical Story:** Explain the text's context and narrative clearly.
- **Identify the Problem/Situation:**

- Highlight the human brokenness, sin, or challenge revealed in the passage.
            - Connect this to the broader *Great Controversy* theme (sin vs. redemption).
    - **Show the Biblical Solution in Christ:**
        - Explicitly connect the solution to Jesus' life, sacrifice, or work in our lives today.
        - Tie the text to Jesus' saving work: "How does Christ resolve this problem?"

Example:
If preaching from Hosea, connect Israel's unfaithfulness to humanity's need for redemption, and show how Jesus, the ultimate Bridegroom, restores us.

3. Proclaim the Gospel Clearly

- **Key Gospel Elements:**
    - **Jesus' Life:** How did Jesus model the solution or reveal God's character?
    - **Jesus' Death:** How does the cross address sin, brokenness, or rebellion?
    - **Jesus' Resurrection:** How does His victory bring transformation and hope?
    - **Jesus' Intercession:** How is Christ presently working in our lives?
- **Anchor the Message in Scripture:** Use verses like:

- John 12:32 – Jesus drawing people to Himself.
- Acts 4:12 – Salvation is through Jesus alone.
- 1 Corinthians 2:2 – "Jesus Christ and Him crucified."

4. Build the Bridge of Application

- **Relate the Biblical Story to Today's Life:**
    - Identify parallels between the Biblical situation and modern struggles.
    - Ask: *How does this truth transform our lives today?*
- **Point Listeners to Jesus' Grace:**
    - Show how Jesus is the source of healing, empowerment, and victory.
    - Encourage reliance on Christ, not self-effort (John 15:4-5).
- **Practical Examples:** Use real-life illustrations that show transformation through Jesus.

5. Balance Rebuke and Encouragement

- **Call to Repentance:** Challenge listeners to turn from sin while showing Christ's grace.

- Example: "God calls us to leave behind this sinful habit, and Jesus has already won the victory for us."
- **Offer Encouragement:** Emphasize that Jesus is with them in life's struggles, seeking to heal and redeem.

6. Structure the Sermon for Transformation

- **Introduction:**
  - Present the text and main theme.
  - Raise the listeners' curiosity by pointing toward the redemptive solution in Christ.
- **Body:**
  - **Problem/Situation:** Expose the need or brokenness.
  - **Biblical Solution:** Connect the solution to Jesus and His work.
  - **Application:** Bridge the Gospel truth to the listeners' lives.
- **Conclusion:**
  - Summarize the sermon's main points.
  - Reiterate how Jesus is central to the message.
- **Appeal:** Call listeners to respond to Jesus personally:
  - "Surrender your heart to Him."
  - "Let His grace transform your situation."

7. Preach with the Holy Spirit's Power

- **Invite the Holy Spirit:** Pray for the Spirit to fill the message, convict hearts, and draw listeners to Christ.
- **Speak with Passion and Conviction:** Share the Gospel as a living, urgent truth that transforms lives today.

8. Uplift Jesus as the Only Solution

- Always come back to this truth:
    - **Salvation is only through Jesus.**
    - **Transformation is only by abiding in Him (John 15:4).**
    - **Victory is found in His grace, not our efforts.**

9. Use Scripture to Shape the Sermon

- Ensure the message flows from the text, not personal opinion.
- Highlight key verses that proclaim Christ (e.g., Isaiah 53:5, Romans 12:2, Philippians 2:5-11).

10. End with Hope in Christ

- Leave listeners with:
    - Confidence in Jesus' saving grace.
    - Assurance of His presence in their struggles.
    - A call to abide in Him for daily transformation.

By consistently applying these practical steps, the preacher ensures that **Jesus is the heart and soul** of every message, leading to Gospel-filled, Christ-centered, and Spirit-empowered sermons.

2

Holy Spirit Our True Source

Praying for Holy Spirit Wisdom & Power Passion in Our Preparation & Preaching

One of the most exciting things in the study is to experience the joy of the Holy Spirit anointing[7] us to preach the word of God. Stephen preached powerfully because he was filled with the Spirit and uplifted Christ at the center of his sermon.[8] The Lord promises us the Holy Spirit[9] to preach powerfully, when we surrender to His will and leading.[10] Zechariah 4:6 declares: *"Not by might (chayil) nor by power (koach), but by My Spirit (ruach), says the Lord of hosts."* The Hebrew word *chayil* refers to human strength or effort, while *koach* speaks to

---

[7] Derek J. Morris, *Powerful Biblical Preaching* (Silver Spring, MD: General Conference Ministerial Association, 2018), 9.
[8] Acts 6:5-8 "full of faith and power"
[9] John 14:12-18 - Jesus promises the Holy Spirit to help us and to be with us forever. (This includes our preaching of the Gospel)
[10] Luke 11:11-13 Jesus promises us "**11** "Which of you fathers, if your son asks for a fish, will give him a snake instead? **12** Or if he asks for an egg, will give him a scorpion? **13** If you then, though you are evil, know how to give good gifts to your children, how much more will your Father in heaven give the Holy Spirit to those who ask him!"

human energy or force—both are inadequate for transforming hearts. True, Christ-centered preaching depends entirely on *ruach*, the Spirit of God, who makes His Word alive and reveals Christ to both preacher and congregation. This requires time in prayer like Jesus did.[11] Derrick Morris says it perfectly in *Powerful Biblical Preaching* "For Jesus, preaching and prayer were intricately connected."[12] This requires us to humbly surrender our human abilities and turn to God in prayer, asking for His Spirit to guide, empower, and bless our message. Right now, God is calling us to that place of surrender—to seek Him in prayer, trusting that His Spirit alone will bring clarity, authority, and life-transforming power to our preaching. Prayer is what brings divine power and humble Holy boldness[13] to our words.

Practical Preparation:

---

[11] Jesus spent time in prayer and solitude because He recognized that He needed to be filled afresh daily and anointed with the Holy Spirit and this is an example for us. (Mark 1:35-39) Derek J. Morris, *Powerful Biblical Preaching* (Silver Spring, MD: General Conference Ministerial Association, 2018), 10.

[12] Ibid. We are called to devote our time to prayer before we preach, recognizing that we need a Divine power to proclaim the Word of God from us. (Acts 6:4)

[13] Paul speaks of this Holy Boldness that comes from prayer in Ephesians 6:19-20 "I will keep speaking in boldly for him (Jesus), as I should. The devil is not afraid to be bold with sin. Why are we shy when it comes to proclaiming our Lord and Saviour who bled and died for us? Preach Jesus!

- **Spend time in Prayer**: asking for the Spirit's guidance and illumination to prepare us to go proclaim the Word. (Luke 4:18, Acts 1:4,5,8)
  - Preacher's Prayer: Lord Jesus fill me with your grace[14]. Fill my heart with your joy and Holy boldness to preach the Word of God.
  - Pray for transformation (Romans 12:1-2) that comes when the Word of God is preached.
- Meditate deeply on the passage, allowing God to speak to your heart before you speak to others.
- Surrender your own ideas and seek the Spirit's direction to focus on Christ and His message.[15]

Key Questions to Pray Over

1. Have I humbled myself before God, recognizing my need for the Spirit's guidance in preparing and delivering the message?
2. Is Christ at the center of my sermon, or have I allowed other focuses to take His place?
3. Have I prayed for the Holy Spirit to make the Word come alive in my heart before sharing it with others?

---

[14] Jesus preached with grace and truth (Luke 4:22) because He was filled with grace (John 1:14) this should drop us to our knees humbly in prayer because we in our own nature does not produce this divine grace. We need the Holy Spirit to fill us with grace for God's people before we preach.

[15] We need to surrender to the temptation to preach our own opinions and traditions and to preach from scripture. The Main points of our semon must be from the actual Biblical text connecting it to the Good News of the Gospel for us to be Christ-centered Biblical Preaching.

4. Am I trusting the Spirit to communicate the message effectively to the congregation, or am I relying on my own words and delivery?
5. In my preparation and preaching, do I create space for the Spirit to work, or do I rely too heavily on structure and human effort?

God's Eternal Love as the Heartbeat of the Gospel

The love of God is the central message of the Gospel and must be the driving force behind every sermon. By recognizing God's eternal love for humanity—demonstrated through Christ's sacrifice and the ongoing work of the Holy Spirit—the preacher is compelled to declare this truth with passion and authenticity. A preacher who has experienced this transformative love will naturally preach it with conviction.

Connection to Preaching the Heart of the Gospel:

Preaching Christ-centered sermons requires a deep personal experience with God's love. The preacher must allow this love to overflow in their message, speaking of Christ's sacrifice and grace, and ensuring that the sermon points to the redemptive work of Christ.

Preaching with Humility

Humility is essential in preaching. It is the preacher's posture before God and the congregation. A preacher must surrender their own wisdom and pride, acknowledging their dependence on God. This humility should be evident not only in the preparation of the sermon but in its delivery, recognizing that it is only by God's grace that the message can reach the hearts of the audience.

Preaching with Authenticity:

True Christ-centered preaching flows from a heart of humility. The preacher must surrender their ego, ensuring that the message glorifies God, not themselves. This humility allows the preacher to focus solely on Christ, allowing Him to speak through the sermon.

A preacher's identity must be rooted in Christ. The sermon should reflect Christ—not personal accolades or ambitions. By aligning their identity with Christ, the preacher finds their strength and purpose. Preaching becomes a call to make Christ known and to point to His life, death, and resurrection.

Preaching from a Christ-Centered Identity:

A Christ-centered sermon is delivered from the preacher's identity in Christ. The preacher's role is to reflect Christ's glory, not their own. Every message must point to Jesus and His work, as this is the essence of the Gospel.

Total Surrender: Allowing God to Speak Through the Preacher

Full surrender to God means yielding to Him in every aspect of preaching—both in preparation and delivery. Every word, every gesture, and every Scripture referenced should point to Christ. The preacher must trust that God will use them as His vessel, submitting to God's will and allowing Him to take full control of the sermon.

Connection to Preaching through Total Surrender: Surrender is vital to ensure that the sermon remains Christ-centered. The preacher must trust in God's guidance and allow His Spirit to lead the message, ensuring that every aspect of the sermon points back to Jesus Christ.

Formula for Fully Surrendering to God in Humility to Preach Christ-Centered Biblical Sermons

Here is the formula to visually represent the process of fully surrendering to God for preaching Christ-centered Biblical sermons:

Sermon Prayer Points

Prayerfully ReRead + Review Your Sermon with these touchpoints below:

Lord Give Me Your Humility (Posture of Dependence on God)

+

Love Fill My Words and Motives with the Eternal Love of God (Heart of the Gospel)

+

Lord allow my Identity to be in Christ (Reflecting Christ in Preaching)

+

Lord I Surrender my life to you God (Allowing God to Lead the Message)

_____

= Prayer is to preach Christ-Centered Biblical Sermons

Explanation of the Formula:

- **Humility**: Acknowledging our dependence on God and humbling ourselves to His guidance.
- **Eternal Love of God**: The Gospel's transformative message, which compels the preacher to share God's love.
- **Identity in Christ**: Preaching from the preacher's rootedness in Christ, ensuring the sermon reflects His glory.
- **Surrender to God**: Allowing God full control in the preparation and delivery of the sermon.

By following this formula, the preacher remains grounded in humility, filled with God's love, centered on their identity in Christ, and surrendered to God's leading, ensuring a Christ-centered message is preached.

3

Loving Jesus before we Preach Jesus

Before we preach Jesus we must come face to face with Jesus

Before we can effectively preach Jesus, we must first come face to face with Him. True, impactful preaching begins not in the pulpit but in the quiet, personal surrender to the love of Jesus. Without this encounter, our words may sound hollow—truth without grace, doctrine without relationship[16].

To preach Jesus is to reflect His grace. We must be aware of our audience and their verbal and nonverbal responses.[17] The people we minister to are already burdened by the pain and guilt of sin. The world does not lack reminders of brokenness. What it desperately needs is the Gospel—grace, peace, healing, and restoration that flow from the cross of Christ. Scripture is not a hammer to crush; it is a balm to heal. The power of God's Word, when delivered through the lens of grace, points the sinner to hope and new life in Jesus.

---

[16] Jesus knew His audience, he spent time with them to understand their needs. Jesus preached to the deepest needs of the hearts of the people. He preached to the concerns that were on their minds (Matt. 24:3; Luke 10:39) Derek J. Morris, *Powerful Biblical Preaching* (Silver Spring, MD: General Conference Ministerial Association, 2018), 12.
[17] ibid.12

Peter's Face-to-Face with Jesus

In John 21, we witness a moment of grace-filled restoration. After denying Jesus three times, Peter's guilt weighed heavily on him. But Jesus, in His infinite love, looked Peter in the face and restored him. Three times, Jesus asked, *"Do you love me?"* Each question was not a condemnation but a gentle invitation to reflect, confess, and return to relationship.

Peter's restoration came through love, not judgment. Jesus didn't shame him for his failure. Instead, He called Peter to love and care for others: *"Feed my sheep"* (John 21:17). Only after being fully restored by Christ's love was Peter ready to preach with power at Pentecost (Acts 2). His preaching was not just informed by doctrine but transformed by grace.

Surrender Before Service

To preach Jesus, we must first love Him. To love Him, we must experience His grace and allow Him to look into our hearts. This requires surrender—laying down our pride, failures, and ambitions at the foot of the cross. Only then can we preach a message that resonates with the broken, because we ourselves have been restored.

Preaching Against Sin in Grace and Peace

The world doesn't need preachers who merely *talk* about Jesus; it needs preachers who *walk* with Jesus. Before we proclaim His name, we must first be loved by Him, transformed by Him, and fully surrendered to Him. Only then can we authentically preach the Gospel—a message that flows from grace, peace, healing, and restoration.

A preacher who is led by the Holy Spirit and abides in Jesus will preach with a heart of grace and peace.

The world needs preachers who boldly address sin, but they must do so through the love of Jesus Christ.[18] The Apostle Paul exemplifies this in his letters. In Galatians 6:1, Paul instructs believers to restore those caught in sin *"in a spirit of gentleness."* He understood that correction delivered from pride, anger, or selfish motives wounds the soul instead of healing it. A harsh rebuke can drive people away from Christ, while a message spoken with humility and love invites them to repentance and restoration.

This is vital because sermons born from pride or frustration can cause lasting damage. A thirty-minute rant might require thirty weeks—or even thirty years—of healing, and some wounds may never fully mend. But a sermon led by the Spirit,

---

[18] Jesus Himself modeled this beautifully. In John 8:1–11, when the woman caught in adultery was brought before Him, Jesus did not overlook her sin, but neither did He condemn her. Instead, He extended grace: *"Neither do I condemn you; go, and from now on sin no more"* (v. 11). He spoke the truth about sin, but His words were saturated with love and peace, leading her to transformation, not despair.

rooted in love and truth, reflects the heart of God: a heart that confronts sin not to condemn, but to restore.

As preachers, let us abide in Christ, walk in step with the Holy Spirit, and speak the truth in love (Ephesians 4:15). In doing so, we will be faithful to the Gospel, bringing both conviction and hope to a world desperate for grace and peace.

Action Steps for Opening Our Hearts to the Love of Jesus to Preach Effectively

1. **Pray for a Heart of Humility and Love:**
   Begin by praying with the words of David: *"Create in me a clean heart, O God, and renew a right spirit within me"* (Psalm 51:10). Humble yourself before the Lord, for *"Humble yourselves before the Lord, and He will lift you up"* (James 4:10). Clothe yourself with *"compassion, kindness, humility, gentleness, and patience"* (Colossians 3:12), seeking to reflect His character as you prepare.

2. **Abide in Christ Daily:**
   Jesus said, *"Abide in Me, and I in you. As the branch cannot bear fruit by itself unless it abides in the vine, neither can you unless you abide in Me"* (John 15:4). Meditate on God's Word day and night, for *"his delight is in the law of the Lord, and on His law he meditates day and night. He is like a tree planted by streams of water"* (Psalm 1:2-3). Allow your mind to be renewed daily: *"Do not be conformed to this world, but be transformed by the renewal of your mind"* (Romans 12:2).

3. **Seek the Spirit's Guidance:**
   Trust the Holy Spirit to guide your message: *"When the Spirit of truth comes, He will guide you into all the truth"* (John 16:13). Walk in step with the Spirit: *"But I say, walk by the Spirit, and you will not gratify the desires of the flesh"* (Galatians 5:16). Pray for boldness and clarity in your words, *"praying at all times in the Spirit... that words may be given to me in opening my mouth boldly to proclaim the mystery of the Gospel"* (Ephesians 6:18-19).

4. **Examine Your Motives:**
   Let love be your foundation: *"If I speak in the tongues of men and of angels, but have not love, I am a noisy gong or a clanging cymbal"* (1 Corinthians 13:1). Preach out of Christ's love, *"For the love of Christ controls us, because we have concluded this: that One has died for all, therefore all have died"* (2 Corinthians 5:14-15). Reflect deeply, for *"All the ways of a man are pure in his own eyes, but the Lord weighs the spirit"* (Proverbs 16:2).

5. **Speak Truth with Gentleness:**
   Follow Paul's counsel: *"Brothers, if anyone is caught in any transgression, you who are spiritual should restore him in a spirit of gentleness"* (Galatians 6:1). Speak the truth in love: *"Rather, speaking the truth in love, we are to grow up in every way into Him who is the head, into Christ"* (Ephesians 4:15). Be patient and gentle in teaching, *"correcting his opponents with gentleness. God may perhaps grant them repentance leading to a knowledge of the truth"* (2 Timothy 2:24-25).

6. **Focus on the Heart of God:**
Look to Jesus, who said to the woman caught in sin, *"Neither do I condemn you; go, and from now on sin no more"* (John 8:11). Embrace His mission: *"For the Son of Man came to seek and to save the lost"* (Luke 19:10). Show compassion like Christ, who said, *"Those who are well have no need of a physician, but those who are sick... I came not to call the righteous, but sinners"* (Matthew 9:12-13).

7. **Use Scripture as the Foundation:**
Ground your message in the authority of God's Word: *"All Scripture is breathed out by God and profitable for teaching, for reproof, for correction, and for training in righteousness"* (2 Timothy 3:16-17). Let Scripture pierce the heart: *"For the Word of God is living and active, sharper than any two-edged sword... discerning the thoughts and intentions of the heart"* (Hebrews 4:12). Proclaim the hope of the Gospel: *"For the wages of sin is death, but the free gift of God is eternal life in Christ Jesus our Lord"* (Romans 6:23). Encourage confession and forgiveness: *"If we confess our sins, He is faithful and just to forgive us our sins and to cleanse us from all unrighteousness"* (1 John 1:9).

8. **Provide Hope and Restoration:**
Preach the love of God displayed in Christ: *"But God shows His love for us in that while we were still sinners, Christ died for us"* (Romans 5:8). Point to the transforming power of Jesus: *"If anyone is in Christ, he is a new creation. The old has passed away; behold, the*

new has come" (2 Corinthians 5:17). Remind your listeners of the healing found at the cross: *"He Himself bore our sins in His body on the tree, that we might die to sin and live to righteousness. By His wounds you have been healed"* (1 Peter 2:24). Share the invitation to salvation: *"For God so loved the world, that He gave His only Son, that whoever believes in Him should not perish but have eternal life"* (John 3:16-17).

9. **Review and Reflect:**

    After preparing, pray David's words: *"Search me, O God, and know my heart! Try me and know my thoughts! And see if there be any grievous way in me, and lead me in the way everlasting"* (Psalm 139:23-24). Ask yourself: *"So, whether you eat or drink, or whatever you do, do all to the glory of God"* (1 Corinthians 10:31). Speak with grace: *"Let your speech always be gracious, seasoned with salt, so that you may know how you ought to answer each person"* (Colossians 4:6).

10. **Seek Accountability:**

    Invite trusted mentors to sharpen you: *"Iron sharpens iron, and one man sharpens another"* (Proverbs 27:17). Lean on the strength of fellowship: *"Two are better than one, because they have a good reward for their toil. For if they fall, one will lift up his fellow"* (Ecclesiastes 4:9-10). Encourage one another in ministry: *"Therefore encourage one another and build one another up, just as you are doing"* (1 Thessalonians 5:11).

4

Meeting Jesus in the Text

When we approach the Bible for preaching, we must recognize that the text is not a lifeless document to be analyzed, but a living Word that calls us to encounter Jesus Christ. First we make the decision that Jesus is the living Word of God and we are biblically called to use the Bible as our foundation.[19] Engaging Scripture involves **listening to Jesus speak through the text**. Christ-centered preaching allows His voice to shape both the preacher and the hearers.[20] True exegesis reveals Jesus as He "speaks" (Luke 24:27), just as He opened the Scriptures to the disciples on the road to Emmaus. **Jesus not only speaks but acts.**[21] Christ-centered preaching must convey this power. The role of the preacher is not to invent or embellish but to unveil Christ in the text.[22]

Ask the Key Question: How does this text fit into God's plan to save us?

---

[19] Bryan Chapell, *Christ-Centered Preaching: Redeeming the Expository Sermon*, 3rd ed. (Grand Rapids: Baker Academic, 2018), 66.
[20] Lewis, *A Lay Preacher's Guide*, 3.
[21] Lewis, *A Lay Preacher's Guide*, 6.
[22] Chapell, *Christ-Centered Preaching*, 66.

Make Preaching connections to *The Redemption Story*. When Preaching Jesus the redemption story helps connect any Bible passage to Jesus. Every sermon should show how the passage points to God's plan to save us, with Jesus as the focus.[23]

Every explanation should point back to His grace, redemption, and character. Preaching Jesus means proclaiming His transformative presence, which brings life (John 10:10).

Preaching is not about us discovering Jesus by our own intellect; it is about allowing Jesus to reveal Himself to us through His Spirit. As preachers, we do not manufacture His presence in the text; we submit to His invitation to meet Him. This truth reshapes how we prepare sermons—with humility, expectation, and reverence. There is a call for humility before the Word of God in prayer and deep study of the Word.[24]

Practical Steps to Connect the Preaching Scripture to God's Plan to Save Us

1. **Identify the Big Picture of Redemption**
    - Review the overarching story of redemption: Creation, Fall, Promise, Redemption through Jesus, and Restoration.

---

[23] Chapell, *Christ-Centered Preaching*, 80.

[24] Meeting Jesus requires a prayerful and humble posture, combined with rigorous study of His Word. This balance allows us to hear Him speak clearly. John Stott, *Between Two Worlds: The Art of Preaching in the Twentieth Century* (Grand Rapids: Eerdmans, 1982), 221.

- Keep this framework in mind as you study the passage.

2. **Examine the Context of the Passage**
   - Understand the passage in its immediate and broader biblical context.
   - Ask: How does this text relate to sin, grace, faith, or God's promises?

3. **Look for Christ-Centered Themes**
   - Identify key themes like sacrifice, covenant, deliverance, forgiveness, or new life.
   - Show how these themes point to Jesus as the ultimate fulfillment.

4. **Connect to the Gospel Directly**
   - Ask:
     - Where do I see the need for a Savior?
     - How does this passage reveal Jesus' life, death, resurrection, or His role as Redeemer?

5. **Trace Promises and Fulfillment**
   - Highlight Old Testament prophecies, promises, or symbols and connect them to their fulfillment in Jesus (e.g., Passover lamb → Christ as the Lamb of God).

6. **Find Jesus in Every Type and Shadow**
   - Use typology: Show how people, events, or objects in the passage reflect Christ (e.g., Moses → Jesus as the ultimate Deliverer).

7. **Show the Human Condition and God's Grace**

- Identify the problem (sin, brokenness) and God's solution (redemption through Jesus).

8. **Use Cross-References to the New Testament**
    - If preaching from the Old Testament, use New Testament verses to show how Jesus fulfills or clarifies the passage.

9. **End with a Clear Call to Jesus**
    - Always conclude by pointing listeners to Jesus as the center of the redemption story and their personal need for Him.

10. **Illustrate the Redemption Story Practically**
    - Use real-life examples, stories, or metaphors that reflect how Jesus' saving work applies to us today.

11. **Test the Sermon for Christ-Centered Focus**
    - Ask: If I remove Jesus from this message, does it still make sense? If yes, I need to refocus on Him.

Hebrews 4:12 reminds us that the Word of God is living and active. It pierces hearts and minds because Jesus, the Living Word, speaks through it. The preacher who humbles themselves[25] before the passage will find that Jesus first seeks them out. When we stand before the text with surrendered hearts, we encounter Christ, who both reads us and reveals

---

[25] To preach Christ effectively, we must allow the text to saturate our hearts and minds, transforming us before we bring His message to others.Stott, *Between Two Worlds*, 221.

Himself. Every sermon must begin with this holy encounter—the preacher meeting Jesus, so that the congregation can meet Him as well.

In Luke 24:32, the disciples' burning hearts testify to what happens when Jesus opens the Scriptures: we meet the One who was, is, and is to come. This moment is the preacher's goal—to prepare not just a sermon, but a pathway for people to meet Jesus through the proclaimed Word.

Who Is God the Son?

The central focus of every sermon must be Jesus Christ—the eternal Son of God. To preach any passage without Christ as its center is to miss the purpose of Scripture. Jesus is not merely an important figure; He is God Himself, equal with the Father and the Spirit. This understanding grounds our preaching in the divine authority and power of Christ. As John 1:1-3 declares, Jesus has always existed as the Word through whom all things were made.

When we prepare sermons, we must not preach a concept or moral teaching alone—we preach Jesus, the visible revelation of the invisible God (Colossians 2:9). He is the One who brings the text to life, for He is the life (John 14:6). Philippians 2:6-8 reveals the humility of Jesus in becoming human to save us. This passage challenges us as preachers: our proclamation must echo the humility of Christ.

To stand before the text is to stand before the Son of God, who reveals Himself so that the congregation may behold His glory and be transformed.

Jesus Christ, Our Creator

Recognizing Jesus as Creator transforms how we approach Scripture and prepare sermons. Genesis 1:26 reveals that the act of creation involved the Godhead—Father, Son, and Holy Spirit—working together. John 1:3 affirms that Jesus, the eternal Word, was the agent of creation. Preaching begins here: acknowledging that the One who created all things now speaks through His Word to recreate hearts.

Paul's words in Colossians 1:16 remind us that everything exists through Jesus. For the preacher, this truth brings authority and confidence. When we preach, we proclaim the voice of the Creator who formed the universe and yet humbled Himself to save us.

Jesus' dual role as Creator and Savior invites us to marvel at His greatness and humility. As preachers, we must communicate both aspects so that the congregation sees Him as the One who made them, loves them, and longs to recreate them in His image.

Jesus' Ministry and Mission on Earth

Every sermon must reflect the mission of Jesus—to reveal God's character, redeem humanity, and call people into reconciliation with the Father. Isaiah 9:6 prophesied Jesus' coming as the Prince of Peace, and Luke 19:10 declares His purpose: "For the Son of Man has come to seek and to save that which was lost."

When we prepare sermons, we must allow the mission of Jesus to shape our message. Preaching is not about entertaining or impressing; it is about faithfully pointing people to the Savior. Whether we preach His teachings, miracles, or parables, everything Jesus did on earth revealed the Father's love and invited sinners to repentance.

To preach Christ is to continue His mission—to proclaim the good news that God is near, that broken hearts can be restored, and that sinners can be saved.

Jesus, the Savior of the World

At the heart of every sermon must be the cross of Jesus Christ. The preacher who meets Jesus in the text cannot avoid His sacrifice, for it is through His death and resurrection that all Scripture finds its fulfillment. Isaiah 53:5 declares, "He was wounded for our transgressions ... and by His stripes we are healed."

To preach without the cross is to preach without power. Jesus Himself said, "I lay down My life that I may take it again" (John 10:17-18). This voluntary act of love demands that every sermon points to the saving work of Christ.

The resurrection further ensures the preacher's hope. 1 Corinthians 15:3-4 confirms that Christ's victory over sin and death secures eternal life for all who believe. When we prepare to preach, we proclaim not a dead Savior but a living One—the risen Christ who transforms lives today.

Jesus as Our Advocate and Coming King

Jesus' work did not end with the cross; He now ministers as our Advocate and High Priest in heaven. Hebrews 8:1-2 affirms that He intercedes on our behalf, applying the merits of His sacrifice. This truth gives preachers confidence—we proclaim a Savior who not only died but continues to work for His people.

Furthermore, Jesus is coming again. Revelation 1:7 promises His glorious return to restore all things. Every sermon must carry this sense of urgency and hope—pointing listeners to the future reality of His Kingdom.

To preach Jesus as Advocate and King is to remind the congregation that He is not distant. He intercedes for them now and will return in glory to fulfill His promises. Preaching this truth stirs hearts to respond with faith and hope.

Conclusion: Meeting Jesus Today

The purpose of preaching is to help people meet Jesus in the text. He is the Creator who made them, the Savior who died for them, the Advocate who intercedes for them, and the King who is coming again. The preacher must first encounter Jesus in the Word before inviting others to do the same. As we stand before the text, Jesus calls us into His presence, transforming our hearts and preparing us to proclaim His message.

The invitation remains: "Come to Me, all you who labor and are heavy laden, and I will give you rest" (Matthew 11:28, NKJV). Every sermon extends this invitation—to meet Jesus, the living Word, who reveals Himself through Scripture.

Action Steps for Christ-Centered Preaching

1. **Approach the Text as God's Living Word**
   - Treat Scripture not merely as information but as God's active, living presence.
   - **Ask**: How does this passage reveal Jesus, the Word made flesh (John 1:14)?
2. **Facilitate an Encounter with God**
   - Pray for the Holy Spirit to make the sermon a space where listeners encounter God, not just hear about Him.
   - **Ask**: How does this message help the congregation experience God's presence?
3. **Focus on Transformation, Not Just Explanation**
   - Prepare the sermon with the intent of transforming hearts, not just delivering content.

- Ask: How does this passage lead people to faith in Jesus as the Messiah (John 20:31)?

4. **Engage in a "Conversation" with the Text**
   - Listen to what the text is saying and allow it to "talk back" as you study.
   - **Practice**: Write questions and observations as you meditate on the passage.
   - **Ask**: Where do I hear Jesus speaking, challenging, or comforting through this passage?

5. **Embody the Presence of Jesus in Preaching**
   - Remember that God's Word is performative—it brings life and transformation into existence.
   - **Practice**: Preach with confidence that Christ is present, alive, and active through His Word (John 10:10).

6. **Connect the Text to Jesus' Revelation of God**
   - Reveal how the passage connects to Christ as the ultimate revelation of God (Hebrews 1:3).
   - **Ask**: How does this text point to Jesus and God's redemptive work?

7. **Let Christ Shape Your Exegesis and Proclamation**
   - Use the text to listen deeply to Christ's voice, just as He opened the Scriptures to the disciples on the road to Emmaus (Luke 24:27).

- **Practice:** Preach the particularities of the passage but always connect to its fulfillment in Christ.

8. **Call for a Faith Response**
   - Design the sermon to invite listeners into belief, trust, and response to Jesus.
   - **Ask:** What does this passage call the congregation to believe or do in light of who Jesus is?

9. **Pray Throughout the Process**
   - Invite the Holy Spirit to guide your study, writing, and delivery so the sermon leads to an encounter with Jesus.
   - **Practice:** Pray before, during, and after sermon preparation.

10. **Remember: The Word Is God's Presence**
    - Preach with the understanding that God's Word is dynamic and alive, bringing His presence into the congregation.
    - **Ask:** How can I let the congregation sense Jesus' power and love through this sermon?

. Christ-Centered Sermon Preparation Templates

- **The "Finding Christ in the Text" Template:**
  - **Passage:**
  - **Context:** (Historical, literary, theological)
  - **Where is Christ in this passage?** (Foreshadowing, typology, direct reference)
  - **Christ's Character Revealed:**

- How does this passage point to the Gospel?
- Application to Today:
- Challenge or Call to Action:
- **The Gospel Connection Template:**
  - **Old Testament Text:**
  - **How does this passage point to Christ?**
  - **New Testament Fulfillment or Reflection:**
  - **How does this shape the listener's understanding of Christ?**
  - **How does it inspire transformation and growth?**
- **The "4P Christ-Centered Outline" Template:**
  - **Passage:** Identify the Biblical text.
  - **Picture of Christ:** Where do you see Christ's character, actions, or presence?
  - **Purpose:** What is the main theological or Gospel-centered truth?
  - **Practical Application:** How does this truth impact the lives of listeners?
- **"Text to Transformation" Flow Template:**
  - **Scripture Reading:**
  - **Big Idea:** State the main Christ-centered message in one sentence.
  - **Breakdown:**
    - **Where is Jesus in the passage?**
    - **What does this reveal about His work (life, death, resurrection)?**
    - **How does it meet our needs (grace, salvation, transformation)?**

- **Life Application:** What does this truth call us to be, believe, or do?

---

2. Activities to Make Sermon Preparation Fun and Interactive

- **The Character of Christ Scavenger Hunt:**
    - Provide a list of Christ's characteristics (e.g., love, grace, justice).
    - Ask preachers to search for and identify where these characteristics appear in specific Biblical passages.
    - Challenge them to build a mini-sermon from what they find.
- **The "Bridge to Christ" Activity:**
    - Take an Old Testament story or passage and brainstorm connections to Christ (e.g., typology, promises, prophecies).
    - Identify how the passage bridges to the Gospel.

Passage Spotlight: In our Preaching Passage we have the opportunity to share how Jesus ministers to:

1. The "who" (characters),
2. The "where" (setting),
3. The "what" (key events),
4. The "how" (Christ is revealed),

5. The "why" (transformational message for today).

David and Goliath (1 Samuel 17)

In the Valley of Elah, a young shepherd named David steps forward while an entire army cowers in fear. Across the battlefield stands Goliath, a giant warrior who mocks God and His people. But David does not see a giant—he sees an opportunity for God's power to be revealed. With nothing but a sling, five stones, and unshakable faith, David declares, *"The battle is the Lord's."* In this moment, Christ is revealed as the greater David, the ultimate Champion who steps onto the battlefield of sin and death. Just as David faced Goliath on behalf of Israel, Jesus faces the giants of our lives—defeating sin, breaking chains, and securing victory for all who trust Him. This story reminds us that our strength is not in ourselves but in the One who fights for us. When we feel overwhelmed, we look to Christ, whose victory transforms our fear into bold, unshakable faith.

- **The Characters:** In David, the shepherd boy who steps forward with faith, we see Christ as the Good Shepherd who willingly steps into the battlefield for His people. David's courage reflects Christ's heart—a heart that intercedes for the weak, stands against evil, and rescues the helpless. Goliath represents the giants we face—sin, fear, and death—that only Jesus can conquer. Even the fearful Israelites remind us of humanity's need for a Savior who fights on our behalf.

- **The Setting:** The Valley of Elah becomes a place of ministry and restoration. What begins as a battlefield of fear and hopelessness is transformed into a stage for God's power and glory. Christ enters the "valleys" of our lives—those places of fear, loss, or defeat—and restores them into testimonies of victory through His presence.
- **The Key Events:** David's confrontation with Goliath points to a greater event—Christ's victory over sin and death. With the smallest of weapons, David defeats the giant, showing us that God works through weakness to display His strength. In Christ's ministry, the cross—seemingly insignificant and weak to the world—becomes the ultimate weapon of redemption and triumph.
- **How Christ Is Revealed:** Jesus is the greater David, the One who steps onto the battlefield of sin and evil not with human weapons but with divine love and sacrifice. Just as David stood in the gap for Israel, Christ stands in the gap for us, taking on our battles and securing victory that we could never achieve on our own.
- **The Transformational Message:** This passage reminds us that Christ seeks to restore our faith, courage, and trust in His power. He invites us to see Him as our Champion, who ministers to our fears, stands for us in our weakness, and transforms our battles into victories. Today, as we face our own "Goliaths," Christ calls us to let go of self-reliance and

place our trust fully in Him. He is already on the battlefield, and the victory is His.

John 15:1-5 (The Vine and the Branches)

In this beautiful passage, Christ reveals His ministry of restoration in every aspect of the story, offering life, connection, and transformation.

- **The Characters:** Jesus ministers to the disciples—ordinary people who, like branches, are prone to withering when separated from Him. In them, we see ourselves—people in need of constant nourishment and connection. Christ, the true Vine, ministers to our hearts, offering Himself as the source of life and vitality. He restores us from spiritual barrenness to fruitfulness.
- **The Setting:** The upper room, on the eve of Christ's crucifixion, becomes a sacred space where Jesus ministers to anxious, uncertain hearts. In the midst of this moment of separation and impending darkness, Christ speaks of abiding—turning a place of fear into a space of hope and promise. Today, Jesus still enters our "upper rooms"—places of confusion, doubt, and fear—to offer His presence and peace.
- **The Key Events:** Jesus' teaching about the vine and the branches is not just instruction; it is an invitation. Abiding in Him restores our broken connection with God and enables us to bear fruit for His glory. Just as the branch cannot live apart from the vine, Christ's

sacrifice and resurrection ensure that we can once again be grafted into His life.

- **How Christ Is Revealed:** Jesus reveals Himself as the Vine—our Sustainer, Life-Giver, and Restorer. He doesn't just offer us life; He *is* our life. Through His Spirit, He nourishes our souls, prunes our hearts, and makes us fruitful. His ministry is one of constant, life-giving connection, where we are never left to wither on our own.
- **The Transformational Message:** Christ seeks to restore us from lifeless striving to joyful abiding. When we remain connected to Him—through prayer, Scripture, and surrender—His life flows through us, producing fruit that reflects His character. This is not about performance; it is about resting in His grace. Jesus ministers to our weariness and self-reliance, offering the invitation to abide in Him and find life, purpose, and growth. The call is simple yet profound: Stay connected to the Vine, and let His life transform yours.

1. The Characters

Explore how the people or figures in the story reflect Jesus and His ministry.

- **Who are the key characters in the passage?**
    - Are they leaders, servants, kings, prophets, sinners, or the weak?

- - What qualities or actions in these characters reflect Christ's character (e.g., David's courage, Moses' intercession, Joseph's forgiveness)?
- **How does Christ minister to each character's condition?**
  - Are they fearful, broken, rebellious, or faithful?
  - How does Jesus show Himself as the Redeemer, Restorer, or Intercessor for those in similar situations?
- **Who do these characters remind us of in our own lives?**
  - What giants, struggles, or temptations do we see reflected here that Jesus can conquer?
  - How does Christ stand in the gap for us, as David stood for Israel?

Example Question:

- *In what ways does the shepherd boy David prefigure Jesus, the Good Shepherd? How does Jesus fight the spiritual giants we face today?*

2. The Setting

Identify how the place or context in the story becomes a space for Jesus' ministry and restoration.

- **Where does the story take place?**

- - Is it a battlefield, wilderness, temple, upper room, or a place of exile?
- **How does this setting mirror the struggles and places in our lives where we need Jesus?**
  - Are there "valleys" of fear, "wildernesses" of waiting, or "upper rooms" of confusion and uncertainty?
- **How does Jesus transform the meaning of the place?**
  - How does the battlefield become a place of victory?
  - How does the wilderness become a place of dependence and trust?

Example Question:

- *In John 15, the upper room is filled with fear and confusion. How does Jesus' message of abiding turn it into a place of hope?*

3. The Key Events

Focus on the central action or progression of the passage and connect it to Jesus' ministry.

- **What are the key moments or events in the story?**
  - Is there a confrontation, a sacrifice, a miracle, or a teaching moment?
- **How do these events reflect the Gospel—Jesus' life, death, resurrection, and victory over sin?**

- - Are there parallels to the cross, redemption, or the power of resurrection?
- **How does God use "weakness" or "insignificant" moments to display His strength and glory?**
  - What do these moments teach us about Christ's victory through humility and sacrifice?

Example Question:

- *In David's small stones defeating Goliath, how do we see Jesus using the "foolishness" of the cross to conquer sin and death?*

4. How Christ Is Revealed

Discover and highlight how Christ's presence, ministry, and character are revealed.

- **Where do we see Christ directly or symbolically in this passage?**
  - Is there a type of Christ (e.g., David, Joseph, Moses), a promise, or a prophecy fulfilled?
- **What aspect of Christ's ministry is seen here?**
  - Is He the Deliverer, Healer, Shepherd, Savior, or Vine?
- **How does this story connect to the larger biblical narrative of redemption?**
  - How does this passage point forward to Christ's work on the cross or His return?

Example Question:

- *How is Jesus the "greater David," stepping onto the battlefield for us and securing victory that we could never achieve on our own?*

5. The Transformational Message

Identify the personal and practical impact of the passage, grounded in Christ's ministry.

- **What is the core message for believers today?**
  - How does this passage call us to trust, surrender, or abide in Christ?
- **What areas of our lives does Christ seek to restore through this passage?**
  - Does He address fear, pride, sin, hopelessness, or spiritual dryness?
- **How does this message lead us to deeper faith and dependence on Jesus?**
  - What does it mean for us to place our battles, struggles, or spiritual growth in His hands?

Example Question:

- *How does abiding in Jesus as the Vine (John 15) transform our lives from lifeless striving to joyful fruitfulness?*

Activity: Making Christ Connections in Any Passage

1. **Choose a Passage**: Pick a passage or story (e.g., Jonah in the whale, Moses striking the rock, Elijah on Mount Carmel).
2. **Answer the Questions**:
    - Who are the key figures, and how do they reflect Jesus?
    - How does the setting speak to Jesus' ministry in our lives?
    - What key events point to Christ's victory, sacrifice, or redemption?
    - How is Christ revealed as the central figure of hope and restoration?
    - What transformational message calls us to trust and respond to Him today?
3. **Write a Sermon Outline**: Turn your answers into a sermon outline that highlights:
    - **Introduction**: Connect with your audience using a relevant story or question.
    - **Christ in the Passage**: Walk through the "who," "where," "what," and "how" to show Jesus' presence and ministry.
    - **Application**: End with the "why"—a call to transformation and trust in Christ.

By answering these questions and following the points, preachers can uncover Jesus as the heart of any passage. This process makes sermon preparation a creative and spiritual journey that magnifies Christ and leads listeners to transformation.

First, *pray and surrender* (Heb 4:12; Luke 24:32), seeking the Holy Spirit's guidance to reveal Jesus. Next, *identify the center* of the passage, focusing on how it points to Christ's mission (John 5:39; Col 1:16-17). Then, *understand the context* by studying the passage's original meaning (Phil 2:6-8; Isa 53:5). Afterward, *see the mission*, connecting the text to Jesus' mission to save (Luke 19:10; John 10:17-18). Finally, *proclaim with purpose*, inviting listeners to meet Jesus and follow Him (Matt 11:28; Rev 1:7). This approach helps preachers faithfully guide others to encounter Christ in every sermon.

5

7 Steps for Preparing and Delivering : Christ-centered Biblical Sermons

At the heart of every sermon lies a situation, a tension, or a problem. Whether explicit or subtle, this problem always connects to the Fall of Humanity (Genesis 3) and the cosmic struggle known as the Great Controversy (Revelation 12:7-9). From Genesis to Revelation, the biblical narrative exposes the root issue: sin (Romans 3:23), separation from God (Isaiah 59:2), and the resulting brokenness in the world (Romans 8:22). As preachers, our calling is to expose the problem (Matthew 5:3), illuminate the need for a Savior (John 14:6), and present Jesus Christ as the only solution (Acts 4:12).

This chapter outlines seven steps for crafting and delivering Christ-centered biblical sermons, emphasizing the significance of each section in proclaiming the everlasting gospel.

1. Introduction: Grab the Attention

Begin with a Compelling Illustration: Start with a vivid story or image to engage the audience. For example, imagine an angel appearing in the sky with a trumpet call, delivering a message of eternal significance to all nations, tribes, and tongues. Such a moment captures the urgency of the gospel and immediately connects with the listener's imagination.

Transition to the Biblical Passage: Bridge the opening illustration to the central text of the sermon. Revelation 14:6-12, the Three Angels' Messages, serves as God's final call to humanity, urging us to worship the Creator and prepare for His return.

Read the Text: Proclaim the passage with conviction, setting the stage for a Christ-centered proclamation. Reading the

Word with clarity and passion invites the congregation into the sacred narrative.

2. Problem: Humanity's Need for Salvation in the Great Controversy

The Biblical Problem: Humanity is deeply broken, characterized by disobedience and rebellion (Romans 3:23; Titus 1:15). Sin separates us from God and leaves us in a state of spiritual poverty.

The Cosmic Context: Situate the problem within the framework of the Great Controversy (Revelation 12:4-9). Satan's deception aims to divert worship from the Creator to himself, exacerbating humanity's estrangement from God.

Humanity's Need: Emphasize the desperate need for a Savior. Only Jesus can bridge the gap between humanity and God, reconciling us through His life, death, and resurrection.

3. Solution: God's Answer in Jesus Christ

The First Angel's Message: Proclaim the everlasting gospel, calling people to worship the Creator (Revelation 14:6-7). Highlight Jesus as both Creator and Redeemer (John 1:3; Colossians 1:16).

The Second Angel's Message: Announce the fall of Babylon (Revelation 14:8), symbolizing the collapse of false systems of worship. Jesus, the Truth (John 14:6), calls His people out of confusion into the light of His grace.

The Third Angel's Message: Warn of the consequences of rejecting Christ (Revelation 14:9-11). At the same time, uplift Jesus' sacrificial death and resurrection as the only way to eternal life (John 3:16; Acts 4:12).

Transition: Conclude with a reminder: these messages are not merely warnings but invitations to experience Jesus' victory over sin and His promise of eternal life.

4. Main Point

Key Phrase: "The Three Angels' Messages are a call to worship Jesus, the Creator, Redeemer, and soon-coming King."

Repeat this phrase throughout the sermon to anchor the central focus on Christ and His work.

5. Gospel Connection: God's Grace in Action

God's Initiative: God's love is revealed through the gift of His Son (Ephesians 2:8-9). Jesus' life, death, and resurrection fulfill the hope of the gospel (John 3:16).

The Holy Spirit's Role: The Holy Spirit empowers believers to live in alignment with God's truth (John 15:4-5). Through Christ, we are victorious over sin and heirs of His eternal kingdom (Romans 8:9-11).

6. Application: The Great Controversy in Real Time

Relevance to Today: Apply the warnings and promises of Revelation 14 to present-day challenges. Expose distractions, deceptions, and the urgency of authentic worship.

Call for Commitment: Encourage listeners to align their lives with the gospel truth. Through Christ's transforming power, they can overcome sin and live as witnesses of His grace.

Transforming Power of Christ: Jesus offers victory and the hope of eternal life (Philippians 2:5-11). The Holy Spirit renews and empowers believers to reflect God's character (2 Corinthians 5:17).

7. Appeal: Call for Transformation in Jesus

Conclude with One Key Statement: "Jesus is the heart of the Three Angels' Messages—He calls us to worship Him, walk in His truth, and prepare for His glorious return."

Invitation: Urge the audience to respond to Jesus today. Call them to surrender to His lordship, accept His redeeming grace, and commit to worshiping Him as Creator, Redeemer, and soon-coming King.

Appeal Song: Choose a song like "Jesus Paid It All" or "I Surrender All" to reinforce the message and invite reflection.

Close with Prayer: Conclude with a heartfelt prayer, asking for the Holy Spirit's transforming power in the lives of all who hear the message.

End with the Blessing: "May the everlasting gospel bring you peace, hope, and the assurance of salvation in Jesus Christ."

Conclusion

Preparing and delivering Christ-centered biblical sermons is a sacred responsibility. By following these seven steps, preachers can effectively proclaim the everlasting gospel, leading their congregations into a deeper relationship with Jesus and preparing them for His soon return.

6

Jesus the Victory in the Great Controversy

At the heart of the sermon lies a situation, a tension, or a problem. Whether explicit or subtle, the problem always connects to the Fall of Humanity (Gen 3) and the cosmic struggle known as the Great Controversy (Rev 12:7-9). From Genesis to Revelation, the biblical narrative exposes the root issue: sin (Rom 3:23), separation from God (Isa 59:2), and the resulting brokenness in the world (Rom 8:22). As preachers, our calling is to expose the problem (Matt 5:3), illuminate the need for a Savior (John 14:6), and present Jesus Christ as the only solution (Acts 4:12).

- **Preach the Universal Longing**: Highlight how every human heart has a void that only Christ can fill. This creates a bridge between the audience's experiences and the Gospel.
- **Expose Satan's Deceptions**: Emphasize how worldly pursuits fail to satisfy the soul and contrast this with the sufficiency of Christ.

Foundational Truth: Every Passage Points to the Problem and the Solution

Scripture unfolds in four essential movements: Creation, Fall, Redemption, and Restoration. When humanity chose rebellion in Genesis 3, sin entered the world, severing the perfect relationship between God and His creation. The Fall introduced brokenness into every area of life—relationships, purpose, identity, and morality. But from that moment, God initiated a redemptive plan, culminating in Jesus Christ, the Lamb of God who takes away the sin of the world (John 1:29).

Every passage in the Bible intersects with this story. The struggles, failures, and conflicts we see in Scripture mirror the human condition—marred by sin and entrenched in the Great Controversy. Yet, alongside every problem, we see glimpses of hope: God's promises, acts of deliverance, and, ultimately, the victory of Christ.

Step 1: Identifying the Problem in the Passage

Key Question: What caused the brokenness here?

At the foundation of every sermon lies the root problem of sin. Whether you're preaching about a historical event, a parable, or a letter from Paul, the problem can be traced back to sin's impact on humanity. Sin distorts God's design, bringing:

- **Separation** from God's presence (Genesis 3:8-10).
- **Selfishness** that corrupts relationships (James 4:1-2).
- **Shame** that erodes identity (Genesis 3:7).
- **Suffering** and death (Romans 6:23).

The preacher's task is to identify the brokenness within the text and help listeners recognize how sin manifests in their own lives.

Example: In Genesis 3, Adam and Eve chose self over God, resulting in separation, shame, and suffering. Their attempt to cover their sin with fig leaves illustrates humanity's futile efforts to fix brokenness without God. Today, we see the same brokenness in our struggles with pride, guilt, and fractured relationships.

Step 2: Framing the Problem within the Great Controversy

Key Question: How does this passage reflect the battle between Christ and Satan?

The Great Controversy reveals that sin is not merely personal but part of a larger, cosmic conflict. Satan works to deceive, distort, and destroy, while Christ comes to redeem and restore.

As preachers, we must pull back the curtain on this cosmic battle, showing how the struggles in the text (and in our lives) are part of a broader spiritual reality. When listeners see their problems through the lens of the Great Controversy, they gain a deeper understanding of their need for Christ's victory.

Example: In Genesis 3:1-15, Satan deceives Adam and Eve, severing their trust in God. Yet God promises redemption: the offspring of the woman (Jesus) will crush the serpent's head (Genesis 3:15). This promise points to the victory of Christ over sin, death, and Satan's power.

Step 3: Highlighting Human Insufficiency

Key Question: How does human effort fail to solve the problem?

Sin exposes our inability to fix ourselves. Human solutions—whether through good works, self-reliance, or knowledge—are insufficient to overcome the power of sin and restore us to God.

As preachers, we must emphasize the futility of human effort to fix brokenness. This prepares the listener's heart for the message of grace and redemption through Jesus Christ.

Example: Adam and Eve's fig leaves (Genesis 3:7) symbolize humanity's attempts to cover shame and guilt. Yet their efforts fall short, revealing the need for God's intervention. Only He can provide a covering sufficient to restore us (Genesis 3:21).

Step 4: Revealing Jesus Christ as the Solution

Key Question: Where is Jesus in this passage?

Every passage ultimately points to Jesus Christ, who is the solution to the problem of sin. The preacher's responsibility is to connect the problem to the redemptive work of Christ—His life, death, and resurrection.

When the Gospel is proclaimed clearly, listeners see Jesus as the answer to their brokenness, the victory in their struggles, and the hope in their darkness.

Example: In Genesis 3:15, God promises a Savior who will crush the serpent's head. This promise finds its fulfillment in Jesus' victory on the cross (Colossians 2:15), where He defeats sin, Satan, and death.

Step 5: Crafting the Transitional Sentence

The transition from the problem to the hope in Christ is critical. This sentence serves as a bridge, shifting the focus from human brokenness to divine redemption. A well-crafted transitional sentence prepares the listener's heart to receive the Good News of Jesus.

Formula for Crafting a Transitional Sentence:

(State the Problem) + "But the good news is..." + (Point to Jesus as the Solution)

Example 1:

- *"Sin separates us from God and leaves us in shame and brokenness. But the good news is that God did not abandon us. He sent His Son, Jesus Christ, to cover our shame, defeat sin, and restore our relationship with Him."*

Example 2:

- *"Like Adam and Eve, we try to cover our guilt with our own efforts, but we always fall short. But the good news is that Jesus Christ came to be the covering we need, offering us forgiveness and new life through His sacrifice on the cross."*

Example 3:

- *"The battle between good and evil is real, and sin often feels like it has the upper hand. But the good news is that Jesus has already won the victory. Through His death and resurrection, He crushed the power of sin and offers us freedom and hope."*

Conclusion: Pointing to the Victory in Jesus

Every sermon must move from the problem of sin to the victory of Christ. By identifying the brokenness in the passage, framing it within the Great Controversy, and proclaiming Jesus as the solution, we invite listeners to experience the transforming power of the Gospel.

Core Truth:

- Sin is the problem, but Christ is always the answer.

Final Thought:

- *"For as in Adam all die, so also in Christ shall all be made alive."* (1 Corinthians 15:22, ESV)

As preachers, we are called to faithfully proclaim the message of hope: Jesus Christ, the victory in the Great Controversy, who redeems, restores, and transforms lives.

Practical Steps for Sermon Writing:

- **Identify a Real-Life Situation:**
    - What are the immediate challenges or struggles in the audience's life?
    - What real-world problems need resolution through Scripture?
- **Understand the Significance of the Need:**
    - Why is this issue important for the listener to address today?
    - How does this situation relate to the broader narrative of sin and redemption?

- **Highlight the Root Problem:**
    - How does the failure to trust God's will manifest in this situation?
    - What are the consequences of separation from God in this context?
    - How can you show that this lack of trust is at the heart of the issue?

2. Preaching the Need for a Savior

- **Emphasize the Human Need for Forgiveness:**
    - How does the issue in the sermon connect to the need for forgiveness of sin?
    - How can you present this need in a way that resonates with the human heart's desire for redemption?
- **Make the Gospel Personal:**

- How does the listener's own life reflect the need for a Savior?
- What biblical story or truth can you highlight to show how Jesus meets this need?

3. Crafting the Sermonic Argument

- **Provide Evidence of Scripture's Relevance:**
    - How does the Bible speak to the current cultural, social, or personal struggles of the listeners?
    - What Scriptures will you use to show that God's word is still relevant today?
- **Compare Worldly vs. Biblical Standards:**
    - How does God's standard differ from the world's standards?
    - What are specific examples of worldly views that need to be challenged by the truth of Scripture?
- **Ask the Right Questions:**
    - What questions does this passage raise that need to be answered?
    - What is God revealing through this text?
- **Christ-Centered Focus:**
    - How does this sermon point to Jesus as the ultimate solution to the problem?
    - How can you show that Christ addresses the need for redemption in a personal and profound way?

4. Making Connections to the Listeners

- **Engage the Individual:**
    - How does this text personally apply to the listener's life?
    - What questions can you ask that will help the listener apply this message?
    - How does this passage speak to their personal struggles and doubts?
- **Engage the Community:**
    - How does this text relate to the church or community as a whole?
    - What collective challenges does the community face that can be addressed by this passage?
- **Invite the Listener to Meet Jesus in the Text:**
    - How can this passage help listeners see Jesus more clearly?
    - In what ways does this sermon allow them to experience a deeper relationship with Christ?

5. Preaching with Hope

- **Emphasize the Victory of Christ:**
    - Even while acknowledging sin and brokenness, how can you emphasize Christ's victory over sin?
    - What Scriptures highlight Christ's redemptive power?

- **Point Toward Restoration:**
    - How does Jesus offer hope and restoration, even in the darkest of situations?
    - What does it mean to find transformative love in Christ?
- **End with the Gospel of Hope:**
    - How can the conclusion of your sermon highlight the hope found in Jesus?
    - What invitation can you extend to the listeners to embrace Christ's healing and forgiveness?

These prompts guide the sermon preparation process, ensuring that the message addresses real-life struggles, connects listeners to the heart of the Gospel, and points to the hope found in Jesus Christ.

Jesus is the Solution

The Invitation to Meet Jesus

When we approach the Bible for preaching, we must recognize that the text is not a lifeless document to be analyzed, but a living Word that calls us to encounter Jesus Christ. Preaching is not about us discovering Jesus by our own intellect; it is about allowing Jesus to reveal Himself to us through His Spirit. As preachers, we do not manufacture His presence in the text; we submit to His invitation to meet Him. This truth reshapes how we prepare sermons—with humility, expectation, and reverence.

Hebrews 4:12 reminds us that the Word of God is living and active. It pierces hearts and minds because Jesus, the Living Word, speaks through it. The preacher who humbles themselves before the passage will find that Jesus first seeks them out. When we stand before the text with surrendered hearts, we encounter Christ, who both reads us and reveals Himself. Every sermon must begin with this holy encounter—the preacher meeting Jesus, so that the congregation can meet Him as well.

In Luke 24:32, the disciples' burning hearts testify to what happens when Jesus opens the Scriptures: we meet the One who was, is, and is to come. This moment is the preacher's goal—to prepare not just a sermon, but a pathway for people to meet Jesus through the proclaimed Word.

Preaching Jesus as the solution to every Biblical situation, problem, or conflict centers on presenting Christ as the ultimate revelation of God's character and the embodiment of His redemptive love. From Genesis to Revelation, the narrative of Scripture unfolds with Christ at its center, offering hope, restoration, and clarity in every situation. Whether addressing the fall in Eden, the wandering of Israel, or the struggles of the early church, Christ is consistently revealed as the answer to humanity's deepest needs and God's greatest gift to solve the problem of sin. The incarnation of Jesus—Immanuel, "God with us"—demonstrates God's commitment to dwell among His people, sympathize with their struggles, and provide a path to reconciliation. His life, death, and resurrection show that the character of God is not one of force or coercion but self-sacrificing love that draws humanity into a relationship with Him. As seen in His ministry, Jesus consistently resolved conflicts by offering forgiveness, revealing truth, and extending grace. This establishes Him not only as the fulfillment of prophecy but also as the practical solution to the moral and spiritual challenges that pervade the human condition. Preaching Christ means highlighting how His person and work address every theme, conflict, and promise in Scripture. For example, Jesus fulfills the justice and mercy of God in the tension of sin and salvation. He reconciles broken relationships, embodies the covenant faithfulness of God, and provides the ultimate triumph over evil and death. His sacrificial love invites individuals to surrender their burdens and trust in His ability to transform lives. Preaching that emphasizes Christ as the solution fosters a sense of hope, challenges listeners to live in the light of His grace, and redirects their focus to the Savior who resolves every conflict with divine wisdom and love.

Who Is God the Son?

The central focus of every sermon must be Jesus Christ—the eternal Son of God. To preach any passage without Christ as its center is to miss the purpose of Scripture. Jesus is not merely an important figure; He is God Himself, equal with the Father and the Spirit. This understanding grounds our preaching in the divine authority and power of Christ. As John 1:1-3 declares, Jesus has always existed as the Word through whom all things were made.

When we prepare sermons, we must not preach a concept or moral teaching alone—we preach Jesus, the visible revelation of the invisible God (Colossians 2:9). He is the One who brings the text to life, for He is the life (John 14:6). Philippians 2:6-8 reveals the humility of Jesus in becoming human to save us. This passage challenges us as preachers: our proclamation must echo the humility of Christ.

To stand before the text is to stand before the Son of God, who reveals Himself so that the congregation may behold His glory and be transformed.

Jesus Christ, Our Creator

Recognizing Jesus as Creator transforms how we approach Scripture and prepare sermons. Genesis 1:26 reveals that the act of creation involved the Godhead—Father, Son, and Holy Spirit—working together. John 1:3 affirms that Jesus, the eternal Word, was the agent of creation. Preaching begins here: acknowledging that the One who created all things now speaks through His Word to recreate hearts.

Paul's words in Colossians 1:16 remind us that everything exists through Jesus. For the preacher, this truth brings authority and confidence. When we preach, we proclaim the voice of the Creator who formed the universe and yet humbled Himself to save us.

Jesus' dual role as Creator and Savior invites us to marvel at His greatness and humility. As preachers, we must communicate both aspects so that the congregation sees Him as the One who made them, loves them, and longs to recreate them in His image.

Jesus' Ministry and Mission on Earth

Every sermon must reflect the mission of Jesus—to reveal God's character, redeem humanity, and call people into reconciliation with the Father. Isaiah 9:6 prophesied Jesus' coming as the Prince of Peace, and Luke 19:10 declares His purpose: "For the Son of Man has come to seek and to save that which was lost."

When we prepare sermons, we must allow the mission of Jesus to shape our message. Preaching is not about entertaining or impressing; it is about faithfully pointing people to the Savior. Whether we preach His teachings, miracles, or parables, everything Jesus did on earth revealed the Father's love and invited sinners to repentance.

To preach Christ is to continue His mission—to proclaim the good news that God is near, that broken hearts can be restored, and that sinners can be saved.

Jesus, the Savior of the World

At the heart of every sermon must be the cross of Jesus Christ. The preacher who meets Jesus in the text cannot avoid His sacrifice, for it is through His death and resurrection that all Scripture finds its fulfillment. Isaiah 53:5 declares, "He was wounded for our transgressions ... and by His stripes we are healed."

To preach without the cross is to preach without power. Jesus Himself said, "I lay down My life that I may take it again" (John 10:17-18). This voluntary act of love demands that every sermon points to the saving work of Christ.

The resurrection further ensures the preacher's hope. 1 Corinthians 15:3-4 confirms that Christ's victory over sin and death secures eternal life for all who believe. When we prepare to preach, we proclaim not a dead Savior but a living One—the risen Christ who transforms lives today.

Jesus as Our Advocate and Coming King

Jesus' work did not end with the cross; He now ministers as our Advocate and High Priest in heaven. Hebrews 8:1-2 affirms that He intercedes on our behalf, applying the merits of His sacrifice. This truth gives preachers confidence—we proclaim a Savior who not only died but continues to work for His people.

Furthermore, Jesus is coming again. Revelation 1:7 promises His glorious return to restore all things. Every sermon must carry this sense of urgency and hope—pointing listeners to the future reality of His Kingdom.

To preach Jesus as Advocate and King is to remind the congregation that He is not distant. He intercedes for them now and will return in glory to fulfill His promises. Preaching this truth stirs hearts to respond with faith and hope.

Conclusion: Meeting Jesus Today

The purpose of preaching is to help people meet Jesus in the text. He is the Creator who made them, the Savior who died for them, the Advocate who intercedes for them, and the King who is coming again. The preacher must first encounter Jesus in the Word before inviting others to do the same. As we stand before the text, Jesus calls us into His presence, transforming our hearts and preparing us to proclaim His message.

The invitation remains: "Come to Me, all you who labor and are heavy laden, and I will give you rest" (Matthew 11:28, NKJV). Every sermon extends this invitation—to meet Jesus, the living Word, who reveals Himself through Scripture.

Practical Action: Meeting Jesus in the Preaching Text

To prepare an impactful sermon, begin by **praying and surrendering** to God. Approach your sermon prep with humility, asking the Holy Spirit to reveal Jesus and transform you through the text. A passage like Hebrews 4:12 and Luke 24:32 can remind us that God's Word is living and active, and through prayer, we can invite the Spirit to illuminate the meaning of the Scripture.

Next, **identify the center** of the passage by finding how Jesus is the focus. Jesus Himself pointed out in John 5:39 that the Scriptures testify about Him. Colossians 1:16-17 emphasizes Christ's central role in creation and existence. As you study, ask yourself how this text reveals Christ's mission and the gospel story, helping the listener see Jesus in every passage.

Understanding the **context** of the passage is essential to uncover its full meaning. Philippians 2:6-8 and Isaiah 53:5 help us understand the depths of Christ's humility and sacrifice. To effectively preach, ensure that you explore the passage's historical and biblical context, understanding how it fits within the broader narrative of Scripture. This ensures the message is rooted in the truth and not taken out of context.

Next, **see the mission** of the text by connecting it to Jesus' purpose of saving humanity. Luke 19:10 and John 10:17-18 remind us that Jesus came to seek and save the lost, and His life, death, and resurrection are at the heart of our redemption. Highlight Christ's mission of love, sacrifice, and salvation in your sermon, helping your listeners see their own need for a Savior.

Finally, **proclaim with purpose** by inviting your listeners to meet Jesus in the text. Matthew 11:28 offers an invitation for the weary to find rest in Him, while Revelation 1:7 reminds us that Jesus is coming again, and every eye will see Him. Use your sermon to extend an invitation for your congregation to encounter Christ through the Scriptures and call them to respond by following Him.

By following this approach, you allow the Scriptures to bring listeners face-to-face with Jesus, inviting them to engage with His redemptive work, experience His love, and live out His mission in their lives.

6

Jesus the Main Point & Gospel Connection

At the heart of every effective sermon lies a big idea—a key phrase that ties everything together, points listeners to the core message, and connects every thought to the Gospel. A sermon without a clear and Gospel-centered big idea is like a ship without a rudder. It may drift, but it will never reach its intended destination. The preacher's goal is to deliver a message that not only informs but transforms, by bringing people face-to-face with the power of the cross.

The Role of the Key Phrase in Preaching

The key phrase is a concise, memorable statement that encapsulates the central truth of the message. It serves as a unifying anchor that keeps the sermon clear and focused. More importantly, it ensures that the Gospel remains the focal point. The key phrase is not just a summary; it is the hinge upon which the entire sermon swings.

The Apostle Paul exemplifies this in his preaching. In 1 Corinthians 2:2, Paul states, "For I resolved to know nothing while I was with you except Jesus Christ and Him crucified" (NIV). Every sermon we preach should echo this conviction: Christ at the center, His cross at the heart.

Practical Application:

- Before finalizing a sermon, identify the one central truth you want your listeners to remember.
- Write it as a short, clear sentence.

- Test it by asking, "Does this point to Jesus and the Gospel?" If not, refine it.

The Gospel as the Anchor of the Big Idea

The Gospel isn't just a section of the sermon; it's the foundation upon which the sermon is built. Every theme—whether faith, obedience, repentance, or love—finds its fulfillment in the Gospel. Preaching that fails to anchor itself to the Gospel offers inspiration but lacks the power for transformation.

Examples of Gospel-Centered Key Phrases:

- On repentance: "True repentance leads us back to the cross, where grace flows freely."
- On salvation: "Salvation is not earned; it's a gift we receive at the foot of the cross."

These phrases are memorable and effective because they remind listeners of the Gospel's central truth: Jesus is the answer to humanity's deepest needs.

Practical Application:

- For every passage or topic, ask: *Where is Jesus in this text?*
- Craft the key phrase to reflect how the Gospel provides the solution or ultimate meaning.

Why Every Sermon Must Connect to the Gospel

We live in a world searching for hope, purpose, and transformation. The Gospel alone provides these answers. Paul boldly declares, "I am not ashamed of the gospel, for it is the power of God for salvation" (Romans 1:16). Preaching that does not connect to the Gospel may educate minds, but it will not transform hearts.

Illustration Example: When preaching about the Prodigal Son (Luke 15), the key phrase could be: "The Father's grace runs to meet us at our lowest and restores us to His family." This connects the parable's message to the Gospel of salvation through Christ's sacrifice.

Practical Application:

- Ensure your sermon connects the listeners' need (sin, brokenness, struggle) to the good news of Jesus' sacrifice and resurrection.
- Use a biblical illustration or story that reflects the Gospel in action.

Crafting a Gospel-Centered Sermon: A Practical Process

1. Identify the Big Idea
   - Ask: *What is the central truth of this passage?*
   - Reduce it to a single, memorable key phrase that connects to the Gospel.
   - Example for forgiveness: "The cross reminds us that we forgive because we've been forgiven."

2. Ask: How Does This Connect to Jesus?
   - Jesus said, "These are the Scriptures that testify about Me" (John 5:39).
   - Every passage, whether Old or New Testament, ultimately points to Jesus and His work of redemption.
   - Example: When preaching on hope: "Our hope is alive because Jesus conquered the grave."
3. Illustrate the Gospel Connection
   - Use stories, biblical examples, or illustrations that connect the big idea to the Gospel.
   - Example: The story of Abraham and Isaac (Genesis 22) points to God providing Jesus as the ultimate sacrifice for our sins.
4. Lead Listeners to Application
   - A Gospel-centered sermon calls for a response.
   - Ask: *How does this truth lead people to the cross? How can they experience transformation today?*
   - Example: Preaching on salvation: "Salvation frees us from sin's penalty and transforms us for eternity."

Experiencing Salvation: The Gospel in Action

Salvation is more than a concept; it's the experience of moving from death to life, from condemnation to forgiveness.

Preaching must communicate that the Gospel is both a gift and a transforming power.

Key Idea for Salvation: "Salvation is God's free gift, made possible by the sacrifice of Jesus, and it transforms us for eternity."

This truth connects to 2 Corinthians 5:21: "God made Christ, who knew no sin, to be sin for us, so that in Him we might become the righteousness of God."

Practical Application:

- Show how salvation impacts daily living, not just eternity.
- Emphasize repentance, faith, and surrender as the response to the Gospel.

Formula for Crafting the Big Idea and Connecting to the Gospel

1. Start with the Text: What is the main truth of the passage?
2. Summarize the Truth: Write a concise, clear key phrase.
3. Ask the Jesus Question: How does this truth point to Christ and His work on the cross?
4. Craft a Gospel Connection: Make the Gospel the foundation of the key phrase.
5. Illustrate: Use a story or biblical example to show the Gospel in action.

6. Apply: Lead listeners to respond in repentance, faith, or renewed commitment.

Example Formula in Action:

- Text: Luke 15 (Prodigal Son)
- Key Phrase: "The Father's grace runs to meet us at our lowest and restores us to His family."
- Gospel Connection: The Father's embrace reflects the grace we receive through Jesus' sacrifice on the cross.
- Illustration: The Prodigal Son's return mirrors our spiritual return to God.
- Application: Invite listeners to come to the cross, repent, and experience God's restoring grace.

Conclusion

A clear, Gospel-centered key phrase makes the sermon impactful, memorable, and transformative. It ensures that Jesus is the center of the message, because He is the center of our salvation.

As preachers, let us resolve, like Paul, to "know nothing except Jesus Christ and Him crucified" (1 Corinthians 2:2). When the Gospel remains the heart of every sermon, lives are changed, and God's Kingdom advances.

Let every message echo this eternal truth: "Salvation is found in Jesus alone. He is the way, the truth, and the life."

6b

The Gospel at the Center

God called us to preach the Word—and that is what I had the privilege to do this year at the Faganofi Seventh-day Adventist Church in Papua New Guinea.

After returning from preaching around the country, I encountered a pastor who claimed that Moses and the prophets did not mention Jesus in their preaching, so we do not have to either. This statement piqued my interest and led me to study Scripture deeply to determine whether we are called not only to mention Jesus but also to consistently point listeners to Him as our Lord and Savior in all our preaching.

Should We Mention Jesus?

In today's evolving landscape, should we mention Jesus when we preach? Some argue that a sermon can be meaningful without explicitly mentioning the name of Jesus. However, by examining the teachings of the New Testament, particularly in the post-Resurrection era, a resounding imperative emerges: we are called to uplift Christ and the gospel in every sermon.

The New Testament consistently appeals to preach Christ crucified. This is not merely a suggestion but a foundational principle of Christian faith. In John 12:32, Jesus declares, "And I, when I am lifted up from the earth, will draw all people to myself." This underscores the centrality of Christ in drawing humanity to the heart of God's redemptive plan. Professor Gennifer Benjamin Brooks captures this truth succinctly: "The need of every heart is the Good News of the Gospel."

Acts 4:12 reinforces this mandate: "Salvation is found in no one else, for there is no other name under heaven given to mankind by which we must be saved." Further, Acts 5:42 recounts that the apostles "kept right on teaching and preaching Jesus as the Christ" daily. Clearly, the center of every biblical sermon is Jesus Christ.

The Essence of Scripture

In John 5:39-40, Jesus admonishes the Pharisees: "You study the Scriptures diligently because you think that in them you have eternal life. These are the very Scriptures that testify about me, yet you refuse to come to me to have life." This passage reveals that the Scriptures themselves testify of Jesus Christ. To omit Him from our preaching is to neglect the essence of Scripture, which ultimately points to Him.

The apostle Paul underscores this principle in 1 Corinthians 2:2: "For I resolved to know nothing while I was with you except Jesus Christ and him crucified." It is through proclaiming Christ's sacrificial death and triumphant resurrection that lives are transformed, and souls are reconciled to God.

The greatest sermons are those that point us to Jesus. The best sermon points uplift Him as Savior and Redeemer.

Eternal Peace

The claim that one can preach without mentioning Jesus departs from the foundational principles of Christian proclamation. Scripture unequivocally mandates the exaltation of Christ in every sermon. As leaders, we bear the sacred responsibility to shepherd God's flock and declare the full counsel of His Word. In fulfilling this sacred duty, let us boldly proclaim the name above all names, for in Him alone is the hope, salvation, and abundant life that our world desperately needs.

As we journey in ministry, may we remain steadfast in our commitment to preaching Christ crucified, for it is through Him that lives are transformed, and souls find eternal peace.

Practical Tips for Connecting the Preaching Text to the Gospel

1. **Identify the Christ-Centered Theme**: Each passage of Scripture contains a thread that ties it to the overarching narrative of redemption in Jesus. For example, a passage about creation (Genesis 1) can be connected to Christ as the Creator (John 1:3) and the Redeemer who restores what sin has broken (Romans 8:21).
2. **Use Typology and Foreshadowing**: Explore how Old Testament stories and figures point to Jesus. For example, the story of the Passover lamb (Exodus 12) foreshadows Christ as the Lamb of God (John 1:29).
3. **Highlight the Problem of Sin and Its Solution**: Every passage indirectly addresses humanity's brokenness and need for a Savior. Emphasize how Jesus' life, death, and resurrection offer the ultimate solution.
4. **Integrate New Testament Fulfillment**: When preaching from the Old Testament, show how the promises and prophecies find their fulfillment in Jesus. For example, Isaiah 53's description of the suffering servant is fulfilled in Christ's crucifixion.
5. **Anchor in the Gospel's Core Truths**: Regardless of the text, point to the core truths of the gospel: God's

love, Christ's sacrifice, His resurrection, and the hope of eternal life.
6. **Illustrate Transformation Through Christ**: Share personal testimonies or historical examples of lives changed by encountering Jesus. This makes the message relatable and demonstrates the gospel's power.
7. **Call for a Response**: Every sermon should invite listeners to respond to the gospel. Whether through a call to accept Jesus, trust Him more deeply, or live in obedience, ensure the application is gospel-centered.
8. **Pray for Guidance**: Seek the Holy Spirit's wisdom in discerning how each passage connects to Jesus. Dependence on God ensures the message is Spirit-led and Christ-centered.

By implementing these practical tips, every sermon can become a channel for sharing the life-transforming power of the gospel. May our preaching consistently exalt Jesus and bring listeners into deeper fellowship with Him.

7

Application for Transformation in Jesus

The Purpose of Application of the sermon is Transformation in Jesus. Its building a bridge from the significance of context and relevance of the Biblical time to today. Preaching is not merely an exercise in explaining the biblical text; it is a call to transformation. The goal of application is to bridge the gap between the biblical world[26] and the lives of today's listeners. Without application, a sermon risks being seen as a historical lecture, detached from the realities of life. However, through Spirit-led application, God's Word comes alive, penetrating hearts and leading to real change. Hebrews 4:12 reminds us:

> *"For the word of God is living and active, sharper than any two-edged sword, piercing to the division of soul and of spirit, of joints and of marrow, and discerning the thoughts and intentions of the heart."*
> (ESV)

Application focuses on this transformative power. When listeners see how Scripture intersects with their daily experiences[27], they begin to grasp the practical significance of God's Word. It moves beyond knowledge into action, guiding believers to grow in Christ and fulfill God's purposes in their lives.

2. Building the Bridge: Connecting the Ancient Text to Present Realities

---

[26] By wrestling with both the original meaning and its application today, we faithfully allow Jesus to speak through the Scriptures into the lives of our listeners. Stott, *Between Two Worlds*, 222.

[27] Preaching should not merely aim to extract abstract theology but must imitate Paul's pastoral care, centered on Christ's activity and love, addressing the congregation's real-life needs. Lewis, *A Lay Preacher's Guide*, 18.

A key challenge in sermon crafting is helping listeners cross the bridge between the ancient biblical text and their modern-day context. This bridge is built with two essential tools: relevance and clarity. Preaching is not merely academic; it is bearing witness to encounters with Christ revealed through Scripture, inviting the congregation into a deeper relationship with Him.[28]

A. Understanding the Original Meaning

Before applying Scripture, the preacher must ensure they have faithfully interpreted the text's original meaning. What was God's message to the original audience? Without this step, applications may drift into moralism or superficial advice. A proper understanding of the biblical context sets the foundation for Spirit-empowered application. As Paul reminds Timothy:

> *"Do your best to present yourself to God as one approved, a worker who has no need to be ashamed, rightly handling the word of truth."* (2 Timothy 2:15, ESV)

B. Moving to the Present Day

Once the biblical truth is clear, the next step is to ask: How does this truth apply to today's audience? The preacher must

---

[28]Lewis, *A Lay Preacher's Guide*, 23.

address real issues—challenges, struggles, joys, and decisions—that people face. These connections make God's eternal truths relevant and compelling for listeners.

For example, if preaching on Matthew 6:33 (*"But seek first the kingdom of God and his righteousness, and all these things will be added to you"*), the preacher can address common concerns like anxiety about finances, relationships, or the future. By showing how this verse applies to trusting God in practical ways, listeners are encouraged to prioritize Christ in their lives.

3. Offering Practical Application: Christ's Fulfillment in Everyday Life

The message of Christ's fulfillment is not merely a theological truth; it is a transformative reality that touches every area of life. As preachers, we must help our listeners see how Christ's presence brings renewal and purpose to their daily experiences. Paul captures this beautifully in Colossians 3:17:

> *"And whatever you do, in word or deed, do everything in the name of the Lord Jesus, giving thanks to God the Father through him."* (ESV)

A. Abiding in Christ

The first practical step toward application is encouraging believers to abide in Christ. Jesus Himself calls us to remain connected to Him in John 15:5:

> *"I am the vine; you are the branches. Whoever abides in me and I in him, he it is that bears much fruit, for apart from me you can do nothing."* (ESV)

Abiding in Christ means cultivating a daily relationship with Him through prayer, Scripture, and dependence on the Holy Spirit. When listeners learn to abide in Jesus, they begin to experience His transforming power in their marriages, friendships, workplaces, and personal struggles.

B. Living Out the Word

True application involves moving from hearing the Word to living it out. James emphasizes this point:

> *"But be doers of the word, and not hearers only, deceiving yourselves."* (James 1:22, ESV)

Preachers should offer clear, actionable steps for living out the message of the sermon. These steps might include:

- Forgiving someone who has wronged them (Ephesians 4:32)
- Trusting God with their anxieties (Philippians 4:6-7)
- Pursuing humility and serving others (Philippians 2:3-4)
- Generosity in their finances (2 Corinthians 9:7)

By grounding these actions in Scripture and illustrating them with relatable examples, preachers equip listeners to put their faith into practice.

C. Overcoming Trials and Finding Victory

Application must also address the realities of suffering and challenges. The promises of Scripture remind believers that Christ's fulfillment gives them strength to endure and hope to persevere. For instance, in Philippians 4:13, Paul writes:

> *"I can do all things through him who strengthens me."* (ESV)

This does not mean life will be free of hardships, but it assures believers that Christ's presence empowers them to navigate trials with faith and courage.

4. Calling for Transformation: Inviting Action

The final step in application is a call to action. This is where the preacher moves from explanation to invitation—calling listeners to respond to the message in obedience and faith. The Holy Spirit works through these moments to convict hearts and inspire change.

Jesus often concluded His teachings with direct, actionable invitations, such as:

> *"Follow me, and I will make you fishers of men."* (Matthew 4:19, ESV)

Similarly, preachers must challenge listeners to respond to God's Word with a step of faith, whether it is surrendering sin, committing to a spiritual practice, or trusting God with a specific area of life.

5. Application Rooted in the Gospel

Ultimately, all application must point back to the Gospel of Jesus Christ. Apart from Him, transformation is impossible. The Gospel reminds us that:

- Christ died for our sins and offers forgiveness (Romans 5:8)
- The Holy Spirit empowers us to live holy lives (Galatians 5:22-25)
- God's grace is sufficient for every need (2 Corinthians 12:9)

By grounding application in the Gospel, preachers avoid moralism and legalism, instead pointing listeners to the power of Christ to change their hearts and lives.

Conclusion: A Life Transformed

Application is the bridge that connects the timeless truths of Scripture to the everyday realities of life. It moves preaching beyond explanation to transformation. When preachers faithfully offer practical, Christ-centered applications, they help listeners experience the living power of God's Word. As Paul declares:

> *"All Scripture is breathed out by God and profitable for teaching, for reproof, for correction, and for*

> *training in righteousness, that the man of God may be complete, equipped for every good work."* (2 Timothy 3:16-17, ESV)

Through Spirit-filled application, believers are equipped to live victoriously in Christ, reflecting His love, power, and presence in every area of their lives. As preachers, may we always remember that true application leads to transformed hearts, renewed minds, and lives surrendered to Jesus.

Formula for Crafting a Christ-Centered Application:

1. Pray for the Holy Spirit's Guidance: Surrender the application to the Spirit, trusting Him to bring transformation.
2. Understand the Text: Clearly interpret the original meaning of the Scripture.
3. Identify Christ in the Text: Show how the passage points to Jesus' life, death, resurrection, and work in us.
4. Connect to Real-Life Struggles: Relate the text to specific, relevant situations your audience faces.
5. Call for Action in Christ: Invite listeners to respond by abiding in Jesus and trusting the Holy Spirit's power.
6. Ground It in the Gospel: Ensure the application points back to Christ's grace, power, and presence as the source of transformation.

8

Call for Transformation in Jesus Christ

The conclusion of a sermon is more than just an ending; it is the final opportunity to solidify the message in the hearts and minds of your listeners. An effective conclusion summarizes the main points of the sermon, reinforces the central message, and guides the congregation toward a clear response. This is where the Word of God is brought to its full expression—moving from exposition to transformation. Faithful preaching should transform listeners, leading them to

belief in Jesus as the Messiah. Preaching becomes Christ-centered when it calls people to respond to Christ.[29] The goal of preaching aligns with John 20:31—proclaiming Jesus as Messiah and fostering saving faith in Him.

A strong conclusion has three essential components:

1. Summarize the Core Message Briefly revisit the key themes and central truth of your sermon. Avoid introducing new ideas here. Instead, remind the audience of what God has revealed through His Word. For example:
    - "Today, we have explored the redeeming love of Christ—a love that pursues us, transforms us, and never lets us go."
    - "We learned that through Philippians 3, Paul shows us the power of surrendering everything for the surpassing worth of knowing Jesus Christ."
2. By reemphasizing the main truth, you anchor the sermon's purpose in the listener's mind.
3. Create a Memorable Statement or Illustration End with a statement or story that resonates deeply and is easy to remember. This could be a quote, a Scripture, or a personal story that ties everything together.
    - A short, reflective illustration: "There was once a man who wandered far from home,

---

[29] Lewis, *A Lay Preacher's Guide*, 5

believing he could find fulfillment on his own. But one day, broken and empty, he remembered where his true life began—in the arms of his Father. The Gospel calls us home to Jesus, where real life begins."
- A powerful Scripture to seal the message: "'For what shall it profit a man if he gains the whole world and loses his soul?' (Mark 8:36). Choose Christ—He is everything."

4. Transition Smoothly into the Appeal The conclusion naturally sets the stage for the appeal. Think of it as a bridge from hearing the Word to responding to the Word. A transitional phrase could be:
   - "Now that we have seen the love and grace of God revealed today, the question remains—how will you respond?"
   - "God's Word has been spoken. Now, it is time for us to respond to His call."

Appeal: Call for Transformation in Jesus

The appeal is where you invite listeners to respond to the message of the Gospel. The goal is not merely to inspire but to invite transformation through the Holy Spirit's power. Here's how to craft a compelling and Christ-centered appeal:

1. Make the Appeal Clear and Christ-Centered Always point back to Jesus as the source of transformation. Avoid vague or generalized appeals. Focus on what

God is calling the listener to do in response to His Word. Examples include:
- For Salvation: "Today, if you hear the voice of Jesus calling you to surrender your life to Him, do not harden your heart. Come to Him, for He alone can save."
- For Renewal: "If you are weary and burdened, Jesus is inviting you to lay it all at His feet. Come, and let Him renew your heart and mind."
- For Action: "If the Holy Spirit is convicting you to step out in faith—to forgive, to serve, to share the Gospel—respond to His leading today."

2. Connect Emotionally and Spiritually An effective appeal engages both the heart and the will. Speak with sincerity, passion, and conviction. Use a tone that reflects the urgency and love of God's invitation.
   - "God is not asking you to come perfect—He is asking you to come willing. He will do the work of transformation. Come as you are."
   - "The Father's arms are open wide. Don't wait another day to experience His redeeming love."

3. Pause briefly to let the Holy Spirit move in the hearts of the people. Silence is a powerful tool during an appeal—allow time for reflection and conviction.

4. Provide a Tangible Step of Response Give your listeners a practical way to respond to the appeal. This may include:
    - An invitation to come forward for prayer or commitment.
    - A moment for silent or corporate prayer where people surrender to God.
    - Encouraging them to make a personal decision right where they are.
    - Asking them to write down a specific step of faith they will take this week.
5. Example:
    - "If you want to surrender your life to Jesus today, come forward, and we will pray together. Don't let anything hold you back."
    - "Right now, in this quiet moment, tell God what is on your heart. Surrender your burdens to Him, and let Him lead you into new life."
6. Close with Prayer Conclude your appeal with a heartfelt prayer that reflects the message and the call to respond. Pray for the Holy Spirit to continue working in the lives of those listening.
    - "Lord Jesus, we thank You for speaking to us today. You see the hearts responding to Your call—hearts longing for forgiveness, renewal, and transformation. We surrender all to You and ask You to lead us in Your grace. In Jesus' name, Amen."

The Impact of a Strong Conclusion and Appeal

The conclusion and appeal are not afterthoughts; they are the culmination of the sermon. When done prayerfully and intentionally, they create a sacred moment where listeners can encounter Jesus personally and make life-changing decisions. Preach boldly, appeal lovingly, and trust the Holy Spirit to do the transforming work.

As preachers of the Gospel, our task is to point people to Jesus—from the first word to the last invitation. When we sum up the message and extend the call for transformation, we partner with God in His redemptive work. Let every conclusion and appeal leave the listener with no doubt: Jesus is calling, and now is the time to respond.

9

Grabbing Attention - Introduction

The purpose of every sermon is not simply to deliver biblical knowledge but to lead people into a transformative encounter with Jesus Christ. A Christ-centered sermon introduction is where this journey begins. Like a doorway to the message, it serves to capture attention, establish relevance, and prepare hearts to receive the Gospel.

1. The Introduction Anchored in Christ

God's Word—from Genesis to Revelation—points to Jesus Christ. Whether it is Genesis 1:1 declaring God as Creator, or John 1:1 identifying Christ as the eternal Word, the introductions in Scripture set the stage for God's redemptive work through Jesus.

A Christ-centered introduction should:

- Capture Attention: Use stories, questions, or statements that naturally connect to the person and work of Jesus.
- Establish Relevance: Show how the listeners' struggles, needs, or hopes find their ultimate answer in Christ.
- Prepare Hearts: Point listeners to the transforming truth of the Gospel.

> Example Hook: "Have you ever felt completely unworthy of God's love? The good news of the Gospel is that Jesus came to redeem the unworthy—people like you and me."

2. Biblical Examples Pointing to Christ

God's introductions throughout Scripture teach us that every beginning is purposeful, clear, and ultimately points to His redemptive plan.

- Genesis 1:1—God's grand opening reveals the Creator, who finds fulfillment in Christ, "by whom all things were made" (John 1:3).
  Preaching Application: Begin with the Creator and transition to Christ, the one who recreates and restores.
- Exodus 3:4-6—The burning bush captivates Moses and reveals God's holy presence.
  Preaching Application: Introduce the awe and holiness of God that ultimately draws us to Christ, the mediator of that holiness.
- The Gospels—Each Gospel's introduction highlights Christ as the center of God's mission.
  Preaching Application: Let your opening reflect Christ's identity as Savior, Redeemer, and Lord.
- Acts 2—Peter's sermon begins by addressing current realities and leads directly to Jesus as the risen Messiah.
  Preaching Application: Start with listeners' questions or struggles and transition to Christ as the answer.

Connecting to Life Through Christ

A Christ-centered introduction connects the text to the Gospel and the lives of the listeners:

- Relevance: Show how Jesus meets the needs of a broken world. Example: "In our search for identity, success, and peace, we often miss that true fulfillment is only found in Jesus Christ."

- Transformation: Prepare the heart to encounter Jesus. Example: "The Apostle Paul says in Philippians 3:7-14 that everything he once valued is rubbish compared to knowing Christ. What are we holding onto today that keeps us from Him?"

Practical Steps for Christ-Centered Introductions

1. Pray for Christ to be Exalted—Depend on the Holy Spirit for clarity and direction.
2. Know Your Audience's Spiritual Needs—Identify how Jesus addresses their specific struggles.
3. Use a Hook That Leads to Christ—Whether it's a story, statement, or question, let it guide the listener toward Jesus.
4. Transition Clearly to the Text—The introduction should seamlessly flow into Scripture, pointing to Christ as the center of God's revelation.

5. Conclusion: Pointing to the Savior

The introduction sets the stage for the central truth of the sermon: Jesus Christ crucified, risen, and exalted. It breaks the hard ground of distraction and prepares hearts to encounter the living Word.

From God's powerful introductions in Genesis, Exodus, and the Gospels to Peter's Spirit-filled words at Pentecost, Scripture shows us that every beginning finds its meaning in Christ. As preachers, let us craft introductions that not only engage the mind but lead hearts toward the life-changing message of Jesus.

> Final Challenge: "As we open God's Word today, are you ready to encounter the Savior who alone brings redemption, purpose, and life?"

10

A Life-long Journey of Uplifting Jesus

Preaching is not a static skill; it is a lifelong journey of growing in Christ and learning to share Him more effectively. As we grow spiritually, we also grow in our ability to proclaim Christ in a deeper, clearer, and more transformative way. Ellen G. White reminds us:

> "It is a law both of the intellectual and the spiritual nature that by beholding we become changed. The mind gradually adapts itself to the subjects upon which it is allowed to dwell." (*The Great Controversy*, p. 555).

This truth reminds preachers that the more we focus on Christ—beholding His character, His Word, and His ministry—the more our sermons will naturally reflect Him. Preaching Christ is not just a skill; it is the fruit of an ongoing relationship with Him.

The Journey of Sanctification and Preaching

Growing in our preaching mirrors the process of sanctification in the life of a believer:

1. A New Creation
   Just as 2 Corinthians 5:17 says we are made new in Christ, our preaching must reflect this transformation. A preacher cannot grow without first experiencing the freedom of the gospel. Preaching Christ begins with personal transformation—a shift from preaching out of duty to preaching from a heart captivated by Jesus.
2. Daily Communion with God
   Ellen G. White emphasizes the importance of abiding in Christ for growth:
   "The closer you come to Jesus, the more faulty you will appear in your own eyes; for your vision will be

clearer, and your imperfections will be seen in broad and distinct contrast to His perfect nature." (*Steps to Christ*, p. 64).

To grow in preaching Christ, we must abide in Him daily through prayer, Bible study, and meditation. Just as a branch cannot bear fruit unless connected to the vine (John 15:5), our sermons will not bear spiritual fruit unless we remain in constant communion with Christ.

3. Learning from the Example of Jesus

Jesus, the Master Preacher, modeled sermons that revealed God's love, pointed to the gospel, and transformed lives. Preaching Christ means following His example:

- Focus on Scripture: Jesus continually referenced the Word of God (Luke 24:27).
- Meet Practical Needs: Jesus preached with compassion, addressing spiritual, emotional, and physical needs (Matthew 20:28).
- Proclaim the Kingdom: Jesus's sermons were centered on the Kingdom of God and His redemptive mission (Mark 1:14-15).

By modeling our sermons after Christ's ministry, we preach messages that are not only biblical but life-giving and transformational.

Building Blocks for Growing in Preaching Christ-Centered Sermons

The same principles for spiritual growth apply to preaching:

1. Prayer – Pray before, during, and after sermon preparation. Invite the Holy Spirit to lead and inspire the message.
2. Scripture – A Christ-centered sermon is grounded in God's Word, pointing people to Jesus (John 5:39).
3. Application – Christ-centered sermons are not theoretical; they call listeners to transformation and action. James 1:22 reminds us to be "doers of the word, and not hearers only."
4. Community – Preachers grow in their ministry when they worship, learn, and fellowship with others.

The more we apply these building blocks, the stronger our sermons will become, not because of our efforts alone, but because Christ works through us.

The Evidence of Christ in Preaching

When we focus on growing in Christ, the evidence will be seen in our sermons:

1. Exalting Christ as Savior – Every sermon leads listeners to the foot of the cross, where Jesus' sacrifice brings salvation.
2. Pointing to Christ's Character – We preach to reflect Christ's love, humility, and truth.

3. Transforming Lives – Christ-centered preaching is Spirit-empowered and produces fruit in the lives of listeners (Galatians 5:22-23).

Ellen G. White challenges preachers to keep Jesus central:

> "Of all professing Christians, Seventh-day Adventists should be foremost in uplifting Christ before the world. The proclamation of the third angel's message calls for the presentation of the Sabbath truth. But this truth is to be presented in the great love of Christ." (*Evangelism*, p. 188).

Lifelong Growth: Preaching Christ and Growing in Him

Growing in our preaching is inseparable from growing in Christ. As preachers, we are on a lifelong journey of becoming more like Jesus. The better we know Him, the better we can preach Him.

Philippians 3:12-14 reminds us of this continual growth:

> "Not that I have already obtained this or am already perfect, but I press on to make it my own, because Christ Jesus has made me His own... I press on toward the goal for the prize of the upward call of God in Christ Jesus."

Preaching Christ is a lifelong calling—one where we, as messengers, grow in our faith and continually point others to the Savior who transforms hearts. By beholding Jesus, we are changed, and so are our sermons.

Let us commit ourselves to grow daily in Christ so that we can preach Him with clarity, passion, and power, leading others to experience His saving grace.

Bonus

Preaching the Sabbath & The Seal of God

In an era when secular priorities and spiritual complacency dominate, the message of the Seventh-day Sabbath stands as a unique and profound truth. The Sabbath, rooted in creation and redemption, is not merely a doctrine but a divine invitation to rest, reflect, and reconnect with God. As preachers of the everlasting gospel, we are called to proclaim the Sabbath truth with clarity and conviction, emphasizing its role in God's final call to humanity. This call grows increasingly urgent as we approach the culmination of earth's history, where the Sabbath will be a pivotal test of loyalty to God.

W.H. Branson, in his powerful article *A Revival of Sabbath Preaching*, emphasizes that "the Sabbath is the great question to unite the hearts of God's dear, waiting saints" (Branson 1938, 85). The proclamation of the Sabbath truth is not optional but central to our mission as Seventh-day Adventists. It is through this message that God calls His people to a deeper relationship with Him, preparing them to receive the seal of God.

Problem: The Forgotten Sabbath

The world today has largely forgotten the seventh-day Sabbath. Modern society prioritizes productivity, material success, and entertainment, leading many to neglect or misunderstand God's fourth commandment. For centuries, the Sabbath has been trampled upon, replaced by human traditions that obscure its beauty and significance. Even within Christianity, misconceptions about the Sabbath persist, and many see it as an outdated relic rather than a living covenant between Creator and creation.

This neglect is not without consequence. Humanity's disregard for God's day of rest contributes to spiritual weariness, broken relationships, and a shallow understanding of God's character. In these last days, as prophesied in Scripture, the Sabbath will once again emerge as a testing truth—a sign of loyalty and obedience to the Creator (Revelation 14:12).

Solution: Jesus is Our Example

The solution to the Sabbath dilemma lies in Jesus Christ. As our perfect example, Jesus not only created the Sabbath (John 1:3; Genesis 2:2-3) but also honored it throughout His earthly ministry.

1. At Creation: In the beginning, Jesus established the Sabbath as a memorial of His creative work. Genesis 2:2-3 records that "God blessed the seventh day and made it holy, because on it God rested from all His work that He had done in creation." This divine rest was not born out of weariness but was a purposeful pause to delight in creation and set apart sacred time for humanity's benefit.
2. At the Cross: Jesus reaffirmed the Sabbath in His redemptive work. When He declared, "It is finished" (John 19:30), Christ rested in the tomb on the Sabbath day, completing the work of salvation just as He had completed creation. His example reminds us that the Sabbath is both a day of rest and a symbol of our redemption in Him.

As followers of Christ, we are called to honor the Sabbath as He did, recognizing it as a gift of grace and a sign of our relationship with God (Ezekiel 20:12).

Main Point: The Sabbath and the Seal of God

The Sabbath carries deep significance in the context of the Great Controversy between Christ and Satan. It is a distinguishing mark of God's faithful people—a sign of loyalty and obedience to Him. In Revelation 7:3, the Bible speaks of God's servants receiving a seal on their foreheads, a mark of their allegiance to Him. This seal is closely connected to Sabbath observance because the fourth commandment contains God's name (the LORD), title (Creator), and domain (heaven and earth), identifying Him as the true God (Exodus 20:8-11).

The Sabbath, therefore, becomes the outward sign of the inward seal—a life surrendered to Christ and committed to obedience. As Branson states, "The final struggle between the forces of good and evil … will be fought over the Sabbath truth" (Branson 1938, 86). Preaching the Sabbath truth is essential in preparing God's people to stand firm in the last days.

Gospel Connection: The Sabbath and Redemption

The Sabbath is deeply connected to the gospel of Jesus Christ. Just as God rested after creation, He invites us to enter into His rest through faith in Christ (Hebrews 4:9-10). The Sabbath points us to Jesus' finished work on the cross and His promise of eternal rest for the redeemed.

- Rest for the Weary: Jesus calls, "Come to Me, all who labor and are heavy laden, and I will give you rest" (Matthew 11:28). The Sabbath is a tangible expression of this rest, reminding us that salvation is a gift, not something we earn.

- A New Creation: Through His death and resurrection, Jesus makes us new creations (2 Corinthians 5:17). The Sabbath becomes a celebration of this spiritual renewal and a foretaste of the eternal rest we will enjoy with Him in the new earth.

Application: Remember the Sabbath Day

The message of the Sabbath is practical and transformative. To preach the Sabbath effectively, we must call people to:

1. Remember the Sabbath: Exodus 20:8 says, "Remember the Sabbath day, to keep it holy." Preaching the Sabbath truth reminds believers to prioritize sacred time with God and set aside distractions.
2. Rest in Christ: The Sabbath is not about legalism but about resting in Christ's finished work. It invites us to lay aside burdens, experience renewal, and grow deeper in our relationship with God.
3. Share the Sabbath: Just as Jesus ministered on the Sabbath, we are called to share God's love with others, inviting them to experience His rest and grace.

Conclusion: A Call to Revival

The Seventh-day Sabbath is a beacon of hope in a restless world. It points us to our Creator and Redeemer, offering physical, emotional, and spiritual restoration. As preachers, we must proclaim the Sabbath truth with boldness and compassion, calling God's people to remember and keep His holy day.

W.H. Branson's words resonate powerfully for our time: "The Sabbath is the great question to unite the hearts of God's dear, waiting saints" (Branson 1938, 85). Let us revive the preaching of the Sabbath, recognizing its role in uniting and preparing God's people for His soon return.

Appeal: Jesus is Calling

Jesus is calling us to remember the Sabbath day and keep it holy. The Sabbath is more than a commandment; it is an invitation to experience God's love, rest, and presence. As we honor His day, we proclaim our loyalty to Him and prepare our hearts to receive His seal.

Will you respond to His call today? Will you choose to honor the Sabbath as a sign of your relationship with Him? Jesus is inviting you to rest in Him, trust in His Word, and share His truth with the world. Let us go forth and proclaim the Sabbath truth more fully, empowered by the Holy Spirit and anchored in His everlasting gospel.

References

Branson, W.H. "A Revival of Sabbath Preaching." *Ministry*, September 1938, 85-86.

Bonus 2

Preaching The Three Angels Messages

Preaching the Three Angels' Messages - Revelation 14:6-9

Introduction: Preaching the Three Angels' Messages In these last days, as we witness the rapid deterioration of values and the rise of false ideologies, the Three Angels' Messages stand as a clear and urgent proclamation of the everlasting gospel. Found in Revelation 14:6-9, these messages are a divine call to worship the Creator, reject false worship, and prepare for the second coming of Christ. The messages are a summary of God's final call to humanity, revealing the stark contrast between the gospel of salvation and the deceptions of this world. As messengers of God, we are entrusted with this vital message, one that cannot be ignored or watered down. We must preach it with conviction, urgency, and love.

Problem: The Global Crisis of Worship In a world consumed by idolatry, materialism, and the pursuit of self, the call to true worship is often lost. Revelation 13 introduces the rise of false worship centered around the beast, leading many away from the Creator. Humanity has turned away from the divine, embracing philosophies that elevate human reasoning over divine revelation. The world is in crisis because it does not recognize the true God and is following after worldly powers that promise security but bring only destruction. As the angels' messages reveal, this spiritual crisis is at the heart of the last great battle between Christ and Satan.

Solution: The Everlasting Gospel and the Call to True Worship The solution to this crisis is found in the everlasting gospel, which is central to the Three Angels' Messages. This gospel calls all people to return to the Creator, worship Him in spirit and truth, and reject the deceptions of false worship. The first angel's message, "Fear God and give glory to Him, for the hour of His judgment has come," reminds us that God is sovereign and His judgment is near. It is an invitation to honor God, not just with our lips, but with our lives, reflecting His character in all that we do. This message calls us to recognize God as the Creator of heaven and earth, affirming the truth that He is the rightful object of our worship.

Main Point: The Three Angels' Messages The Three Angels' Messages encompass the entire scope of God's final appeal to humanity:

1. The First Angel's Message (Revelation 14:6-7) - A call to worship the Creator and honor His sovereignty. It declares that the judgment has begun, and all are invited to fear God and give glory to Him.
    - Gospel Connection: The first angel's message points to the Creator's redemptive work in Christ. Jesus is the Creator who, by His death and resurrection, reclaims the world and offers salvation to all.
2. The Second Angel's Message (Revelation 14:8) - A warning about the fall of Babylon, a symbol of false religious systems that lead people astray. This message invites believers to reject counterfeit worship and the corrupt practices of Babylon.
    - Gospel Connection: Jesus came to deliver us from the bondage of false systems and bring us into the truth of His salvation. The second angel's message calls us to separate from worldly practices and embrace the purity of the gospel.
3. The Third Angel's Message (Revelation 14:9-11) - A stern warning against the worship of the beast and its image, emphasizing the eternal consequences of choosing false worship. This message is a call to perseverance and faithfulness, especially for those who endure the trials of the last days.

- Gospel Connection: The third angel's message is not just a warning, but a call to perseverance in faith, trusting in Christ's victory over sin. It encourages us to stand firm, knowing that Jesus has already overcome the enemy.

Application: Responding to the Call of the Angels The call of the Three Angels' Messages requires a response. To preach these messages effectively, we must call people to:

1. Worship the Creator: We must recognize God as the Creator and Redeemer, choosing to honor Him above all else.
2. Reject False Worship: We must be discerning, rejecting the empty promises of this world and aligning our lives with the truth of God's Word.
3. Endure in Faith: We must persevere in faith, trusting in Jesus' sacrifice and standing firm in the hope of His soon return.

Conclusion: A Call to Proclaim the Everlasting Gospel The Three Angels' Messages are more than a warning—they are a powerful proclamation of God's love, truth, and justice. They reveal God's urgent call to His people to return to Him, to worship Him in spirit and truth, and to prepare for His soon return. As preachers of the everlasting gospel, we are called to proclaim these messages with urgency, clarity, and compassion. The world needs to hear this message now more than ever, and we, as God's messengers, must not shrink back from delivering it.

Appeal: Will You Proclaim the Three Angels' Messages? Jesus is calling us to share His gospel message with a world in desperate need of truth. Will you respond to His call and become a herald of the Three Angels' Messages? Will you commit to worshiping the Creator, rejecting false worship, and enduring in faith? The time is short, and the message is urgent. Let us go forth, empowered by the Holy Spirit, to proclaim God's final call to the world.

Appendix :

Christ Centered Biblical Sermons on Biblical Teachings

Sermon 1

The Living Word

"preach the word; be ready in season and out of season."

2 Timothy 4:2

What is the Bible?

We are living in an age where information is abundant, but truth seems increasingly elusive. Every day, we are bombarded by opinions, ideas, and philosophies. From social media to the news, everyone has something to say, but how do we know what is truly the word of life? How do we know which message leads us to eternal peace? The answer is simple: Preach the Word of God.

The Bible is more than just a collection of ancient writings; it is the living Word of God, and when we preach it, we are preaching Jesus Christ Himself. The apostle Paul charges us in 2 Timothy 4:2 to "preach the word; be ready in season and out of season." This is not just a directive for preachers behind a pulpit; it's a call to all believers to share the gospel of Jesus Christ wherever we go.

In a world full of noise and confusion, the Word of God is the one true source of life. But why does the Word matter so much? Let's explore this together.

Problem:

The Great Controversy and Satan's Deception

You see, there's a reason why preaching the Word of God is under attack. The Bible warns us that there's an enemy who seeks to deceive us and lead us astray. Satan, the great accuser, doesn't want us to understand or proclaim the truth. His mission is to distort God's Word, to silence its truth, and to turn our focus away from the life-changing message of Jesus Christ.

In the Great Controversy, we find the cosmic battle between truth and lies. In Genesis, Satan deceived Eve with the words, "Did God really say?" And today, he continues to question the authority and relevance of God's Word in our lives. He whispers lies that the Bible is outdated, irrelevant, or hard to understand. He tries to convince us that we don't need to preach the Word, that we can rely on our own wisdom or follow the trends of society.

Satan wants everything except the Word of God being preached because the Word is powerful. It is "alive and active, sharper than any double-edged sword" (Hebrews 4:12). The Word of God has the power to convict hearts, transform lives, and reveal the truth of Jesus Christ. Satan knows that when the Word is preached in its fullness, the gates of hell cannot prevail against it.

But, there is good news. While Satan works tirelessly to silence the truth, God has given us a mission: to preach the Word. And we're not left alone in this mission. Jesus Himself is the Word, and He equips us with the power of the Holy Spirit to proclaim the good news of salvation to the world.

Solution:

Preaching the Word is Preaching Jesus Christ

Now, let's move to the solution—what is the remedy for this deception? How do we counter the lies of the enemy? The solution is simple: Preach the Word of God.

The Bible is the ultimate revelation of God's will, and it reveals Jesus Christ, the Savior of the world. The Word became flesh and dwelt among us (John 1:14). When we preach the Word, we are preaching Jesus. Every page of the Bible points to Him—whether it's the prophecies of the Old Testament or the life-giving words of the New Testament.

In 2 Timothy 3:16-17, Paul writes, "All Scripture is breathed out by God and profitable for teaching, for reproof, for correction, and for training in righteousness, that the man of God may be complete, equipped for every good work." The Word of God is not just a collection of good advice; it is the authoritative, divine revelation of God's will, and it is what equips us for life.

As Adventists, we believe the Bible is God's inspired Word, and it holds the answers to life's biggest questions: Who is God? How can we be saved? How do we live according to God's will? And, most importantly, how do we experience the love of Jesus? When we preach the Bible, we are preaching the message of salvation through Jesus Christ.

Remember, the Bible is not just a book of rules or a historical document; it is a love letter from God to us. It reveals His character, His purposes, and His plan for salvation. When we preach the Word, we are pointing people to Jesus—the Lamb who takes away the sin of the world.

The Gospel is the heart of the Bible. The story of the fall of humanity, the life, death, and resurrection of Jesus, and the promise of His second coming are all woven throughout Scripture. The Bible tells us that through Jesus, we can experience redemption, healing, and eternal life.

Jesus said, "I am the way, the truth, and the life. No one comes to the Father except through Me" (John 14:6). When we preach the Word of God, we are inviting people into the life-giving relationship with Jesus, the Savior who died for our sins and rose again to give us new life.

Main Point:

Preaching the Word of God is Preaching Jesus Christ.

The Word of God is not merely a set of teachings or moral guidelines—it is the direct revelation of Jesus Christ. Through every verse and every passage, we encounter Jesus, our Savior, who is the fulfillment of all Scripture. Preaching the Word is not just about sharing knowledge; it's about proclaiming Jesus as the central message of the Bible and the hope for the world.

Gospel Connection:

The Gospel is woven throughout the fabric of Scripture. From Genesis to Revelation, the Word points to the redemptive work of Jesus. In the Old Testament, we see glimpses of Jesus in prophecies and symbols. In the Gospels, we witness His life, death, and resurrection. In the Epistles, we learn how His work transforms our lives and equips us for ministry. Preaching the Word is preaching the good news that Jesus saves, that He is the Lamb of God who takes away the sin of the world (John 1:29), and that through Him, we have eternal life.

Application:

So, what does this mean for us today?

1. Commit to Preaching the Word: Whether you're a pastor, a teacher, or a layperson, we are all called to share the Word of God. This doesn't just mean standing behind a pulpit; it means living out the Gospel in our words, actions, and relationships. Share the good news with your neighbors, coworkers, and friends. Use the Word as your foundation for every conversation.
2. Study the Word: If we are to preach the Word, we must know the Word. Make time to study the Bible daily. Let it dwell in you richly, and allow the Holy Spirit to reveal its truths to you.
3. Live the Word: The most powerful way to preach the Word is by living it out. Let the message of Jesus

transform your life. Be a living example of the power of the Gospel.
4. Trust the Holy Spirit: Preaching the Word is not just about our efforts; it's about the Holy Spirit working through us. Trust that the Spirit will guide your words and empower your witness.

Conclusion:

In conclusion, the world needs to hear the Word of God, now more than ever. We are called to proclaim the message of Jesus Christ, the Word made flesh. As we preach, we invite others into the transformative love and grace that Jesus offers. We stand firm in the truth that the Word of God is alive, powerful, and life-changing.

Appeal:

I want to challenge each of us today: Will we answer the call to preach the Word? Will we commit to sharing the Gospel, the truth of Jesus Christ, in every area of our lives? Let's be faithful in preaching the Word, trusting that through it, lives will be changed, hearts will be transformed, and the kingdom of God will be advanced.

If you feel called to commit to preaching the Word, whether through your words or actions, I invite you to stand with me now as we dedicate ourselves to this important task.

Let's pray together, asking God to give us the courage and wisdom to proclaim His Word in season and out of season.

Amen.

Sermon 2

The Trinity

The Journey from Creation to Redemption

Introduction:

We worship one God: the Father, the Son, and the Holy Spirit—three co-eternal persons, united in love and purpose.

While the word "Trinity" is not found in the Bible, the concept is deeply embedded in Scripture. The Trinity is not just a theological concept; it is the foundation of our faith, as it reveals who God is and how He works in the world. Today, we will explore the Father, Son, and Holy Spirit and their united role in our salvation, transformation, and relationship with God.

Scripture to consider:

- John 10:30 – *"I and My Father are one."*
- Matthew 28:19 – *"Go...make disciples of all nations, baptizing them in the name of the Father, and of the Son, and of the Holy Spirit."*
- John 14:16-17 – *"And I will pray the Father, and He will give you another Helper, that He may abide with you forever, the Spirit of truth..."*

As we explore this mystery, we need to understand that the Trinity is not just a theological point but the very essence of the Gospel itself. It is through the unity of the Father, Son, and Holy Spirit that salvation and transformation are made possible for us.

Problem: Sin and the Need for the Trinity's Intervention

The greatest problem in humanity is sin: our separation from God, the Creator. From the beginning, God created us in His image for fellowship with Him, but sin entered the world, and with it, death, destruction, and disunity. As a result, we are unable to restore this broken relationship on our own.

Scripture to consider:

- Romans 3:23 – *"For all have sinned and fall short of the glory of God."*
- Romans 5:12 – *"Therefore, just as through one man sin entered the world, and death through sin, and thus death spread to all men, because all sinned."*

This is the heart of the Great Controversy between Christ and Satan, where Satan seeks to distort and destroy the relationship between humanity and the Triune God. But God, in His infinite love, has made a way for us to be reconciled, and He does so through the work of the Father, Son, and Holy Spirit.

Scripture to consider:

- 1 Peter 5:8 – *"Be sober, be vigilant; because your adversary the devil walks about like a roaring lion, seeking whom he may devour."*
- Revelation 12:4-9 – *"The great dragon was cast out...he deceives the whole world..."*

Solution: The Triune God's Plan of Redemption

God's solution to sin and separation is found in the Trinity's collaborative plan of salvation. God the Father, in His love, sent His Son to redeem us. God the Son, Jesus Christ, became human, lived a sinless life, died on the cross, and rose again to offer forgiveness and eternal life. God the Holy Spirit empowers and transforms us, making us new creations in Christ.

Scripture to consider:

- John 3:16 – *"For God so loved the world that He gave His only begotten Son, that whoever believes in Him should not perish but have everlasting life."*
- Acts 4:12 – *"Nor is there salvation in any other, for there is no other name under heaven given among men by which we must be saved."*
- John 14:16-17 – *"And I will pray the Father, and He will give you another Helper, that He may abide with you forever, the Spirit of truth..."*

Main Point: Uplift Jesus Christ Through the Unity of the Trinity

The ultimate goal of preaching the Trinity is to uplift Jesus Christ, as He is the center of God's plan of salvation. The Father sends the Son to die for us; the Son submits to the Father's will and accomplishes the work of salvation; the Holy Spirit comes to indwell and empower believers, guiding them into truth. The Triune God works in perfect unity for our redemption.

Key Phrase: "One God, Three Persons—One Savior, Jesus Christ."
As we preach the Trinity, we must remember that each Person of the Godhead is essential to the salvation and transformation we experience in Christ. The Father's love, the Son's sacrifice, and the Holy Spirit's empowerment all work together for our good.

Gospel Connection: God's Grace Through the Triune Godhead

The Gospel is the good news of the Trinity in action. God the Father's love for us prompted Him to send Jesus, His Son, to die on our behalf. Through Jesus' life, death, and resurrection, we receive grace and mercy. The Holy Spirit is sent to live in us, transforming our hearts and minds, empowering us to live for Christ.

Scripture to consider:

- Ephesians 2:8-9 – *"For by grace you have been saved through faith, and that not of yourselves; it is the gift of God, not of works, lest anyone should boast."*
- Romans 8:9-11 – *"But you are not in the flesh but in the Spirit, if indeed the Spirit of God dwells in you. Now if anyone does not have the Spirit of Christ, he is not His."*

In this, we see the love of the Father, the grace of the Son, and the transformative power of the Holy Spirit at work in us. It is through the Triune God that we are made whole, and it is through Jesus Christ that we experience salvation.

Application: Living in the Power of the Triune God

As we reflect on the work of the Trinity in our lives, we must ask ourselves: Are we allowing the Holy Spirit to work in us, drawing us closer to the Father and the Son? The Trinity is not just a doctrine to understand—it is a reality to experience. We are called to live in the unity of the Father, Son, and Holy Spirit, surrendering our lives to God's transformative power.

Scripture to consider:

- Colossians 1:24-29 – *"To them God willed to make known what are the riches of the glory of this mystery among the Gentiles: which is Christ in you, the hope of glory."*
- 2 Corinthians 5:17 – *"Therefore, if anyone is in Christ, he is a new creation; old things have passed away; behold, all things have become new."*

The Holy Spirit empowers us to live the Christian life, guiding us into all truth and making us more like Jesus. As we yield to the Holy Spirit, we experience the transformative power of the Trinity in our daily lives.

Appeal: A Call for Transformation in the Name of the Trinity

As we conclude, I invite you to reflect on the Trinity's work in your life. Do you know God the Father's love? Have you accepted Jesus Christ as your Savior? Are you allowing the Holy Spirit to guide and transform you? Today is the day to experience the power and love of the Triune God in your life.

Scripture to consider:

- Philippians 2:5-11 – *"Let this mind be in you which was also in Christ Jesus..."*
- Romans 12:1-2 – *"I beseech you therefore, brethren, by the mercies of God, that you present your bodies a living sacrifice, holy, acceptable to God, which is your reasonable service."*

Call to action:
Let us surrender ourselves to the transforming power of the

Father, the Son, and the Holy Spirit. May we live in unity with the Triune God, reflecting His love and grace to a world in desperate need of hope.

Closing Prayer:
Father, Son, and Holy Spirit, we thank You for the gift of salvation through Your perfect unity. Help us to live in the power of Your love and grace. May we honor You in all we do, and may our lives be a testimony to the world of the transformative power of the Triune God. In Jesus' name, Amen.

Sermon 3

The Creator who Redeems

The Journey from Creation to Redemption

Text: John 12:32 – "And I, if I be lifted up from the earth, will draw all men unto me."

1. Introduction:

Grab Attention: "In the beginning, God created the heavens and the earth..." (Genesis 1:1). These words mark the beginning of time, space, and life itself. In the act of creation, God laid the foundation of His ultimate plan—His redemptive work in Jesus Christ.

- We all wonder about our origins: Where did we come from? Why are we here? How did this world come to be?
- Today, as we reflect on the six days of creation, we will see not only the miraculous design of the world but also how the Creator is drawing us back to Himself through the redeeming work of Christ.

Transition to the Passage:

- Let's explore together the six days of creation, seeing how each day points to the Creator who is also the Redeemer, who was lifted up on the cross to draw all men to Himself.

Read Genesis 1:1-2:3 with Passion and Conviction:

- Read the creation account with emphasis on God's intentional and personal involvement in each part of creation.

2. The Problem (Sin and the Great Controversy):

- What Is the Problem? Humanity's fall into sin disrupted the perfect world God had created. Through disobedience, Adam and Eve fell from grace, introducing sin, suffering, and death into God's perfect creation (Genesis 3:6-19).
- The problem of sin is at the heart of the Great Controversy. Satan's rebellion began before humanity,

and through sin, he aimed to destroy God's beautiful creation.

Scripture on the Problem of Sin:

- Romans 3:23: "For all have sinned and fall short of the glory of God."
- 1 Peter 5:8: "Be alert and of sober mind. Your enemy the devil prowls around like a roaring lion looking for someone to devour."

The Need for a Savior:

- God's creation was good, but humanity's sin marred it. The solution to this problem is Christ—Jesus, the Creator, is also the Redeemer.

3. The Solution (Christ's Work as Creator and Redeemer):

- What Does the Text Say About God's Actions?
- Every day of creation points to the wisdom, creativity, and purpose of God. Jesus, as part of the Godhead, was actively involved in creation (John 1:3, Colossians 1:16), and through His redemptive act on the cross, He made it possible for us to be reconciled to God.

Genesis 1: The Creator's Work:

- Day 1 (Light): "God said, 'Let there be light.'" (Genesis 1:3)

- - Jesus is the Light of the World (John 8:12). He brought light into the world at creation and, through His sacrifice, He shines the light of salvation into the darkness of sin.
- Day 2 (Sky and Waters): "Let there be a vault between the waters to separate water from water." (Genesis 1:6)
  - In the same way, Christ came to separate us from the powers of sin and darkness (Romans 6:3-11). He is the Great Divider, setting apart His people for His glory.
- Day 3 (Land, Sea, and Vegetation): "Let the water under the sky be gathered to one place, and let dry ground appear." (Genesis 1:9)
  - Jesus, through His death, brings life from the earth (John 12:24). Just as the earth was separated from the waters, Christ's sacrifice separated us from the bondage of sin, bringing forth the fruits of righteousness.
- Day 4 (Sun, Moon, and Stars): "Let there be lights in the vault of the sky to separate the day from the night..." (Genesis 1:14)
  - Jesus, as the Light of the World, came to guide us out of the darkness. As He was lifted up on the cross, the world was filled with His glory, giving us eternal light (John 1:9).
- Day 5 (Living Creatures in Water and Air): "Let the water teem with living creatures, and let birds fly

above the earth across the vault of the sky." (Genesis 1:20)
- ○ Jesus came to give life—abundant life, to all who are thirsty and hungry for His presence (John 10:10). As He breathed life into the world through creation, He breathes life into us spiritually (John 20:22).
- Day 6 (Land Animals and Humans): "Let us make man in our image, in our likeness..." (Genesis 1:26)
  - ○ This day points directly to Jesus, the Creator, who, in the fullness of time, would take on human flesh and walk among us (John 1:14). His incarnation was the ultimate expression of God's image, and He redeems us to restore His image in us (Romans 8:29).

The Seventh Day (Rest): "By the seventh day, God had finished the work He had been doing; so on the seventh day He rested from all His work." (Genesis 2:2)

- Jesus invites us into the rest He provides through His salvation. He is our true rest, the fulfillment of the Sabbath (Matthew 11:28-30).

4. Main Point (Key Phrase):

"In the Beginning and the End: The Creator Who Redeems"

- Repeated throughout the sermon, this key phrase will emphasize the dual role of Jesus as both the Creator and Redeemer, who began the work of creation and completed it through His redemptive act on the cross.

5. Gospel Connection (God's Grace & Redemption):

- The ultimate Good News is that the same God who created the universe, who spoke everything into existence, is the one who came to save us through Jesus Christ. God's grace in creation is mirrored in His grace through the cross.

Transition to the Gospel:

- Just as God created light, life, and order out of chaos, He can bring life and order into our hearts through the power of Jesus Christ. The Creator who spoke the world into existence is the same one who offers us salvation.

Scripture Connection:

- John 1:3-4: "Through Him all things were made; without Him nothing was made that has been made. In Him was life, and that life was the light of all mankind."
- Colossians 1:16: "For in Him all things were created: things in heaven and on earth, visible and invisible..."

6. Application (Bridge from Biblical Time to Today):

- Apply the Problem to Today: The same sin that disrupted creation in Genesis still affects our world today. We see brokenness, darkness, and disorder. But there is hope because Jesus, the Creator, entered into this world to redeem it.

Application to the Audience:

- Jesus calls us to be co-creators with Him, taking part in His work of redemption and restoration. Through His Spirit, He empowers us to bring light into the world, order into the chaos, and life into the deadness of sin.

Transformation through the Holy Spirit:

- The Holy Spirit works in our hearts, just as He hovered over the waters at the beginning of creation, bringing about transformation (2 Corinthians 5:17).

7. Appeal (Call for Transformation):

Closing Statement:

- "The Creator who made the heavens and the earth has now made a way for you to be part of His redemptive work. Will you surrender your heart to the Creator and Redeemer today?"

Invitation:

- I invite you to accept Jesus, the Creator, and Redeemer, into your life. Let Him transform you from the inside out, just as He transformed the earth during the creation week.

Prayer for Transformation:

- Ask the congregation to bow their heads and pray for the Creator's transformative power to enter their hearts and make them new, drawing them closer to the Savior who created and redeemed them.

In this sermon, each day of creation serves as a backdrop to the central message of Jesus Christ, who is both the Creator and Redeemer, calling His people to rest in Him and trust in His redemptive work.

Sermon 4

Redeemed & Restored

The Journey from Creation to Redemption

Introduction:

Life often feels like a jumbled contradiction. We are capable of great kindness, yet at times, we act out of frustration or selfishness. Why is this? Why do we, as human beings created in the image of God, still wrestle with evil tendencies, suffering, and brokenness? The Bible offers profound answers to these questions. It reveals to us the truth about our origins—how we were created in God's perfect image, yet fell into sin, marring that image and becoming separated from our Creator. Yet, the Bible also reveals the hope of redemption through Jesus Christ.

John 12:32 invites us to lift up Jesus, for He is the solution to the world's deepest problem: the fall of humanity. Jesus, lifted up on the cross, draws us to Himself, offering us the restoration and redemption we so desperately need.

Humanity's Origins: Created in God's Image

In **Genesis 1:26-27**, we learn that humanity was created in the image of God. We are not accidents of nature; we were intentionally and purposefully created by a loving Creator. God formed us with individuality, with the ability to think, choose, and live. Unlike the rest of creation, humanity alone was made to reflect God's image and character, entrusted with dominion over the earth, and called to live in loving relationship with God and each other.

We were created as indivisible beings—body, mind, and spirit—dependent upon God for life, breath, and everything else. But our story doesn't stop here.

2. The Fall: How Humanity Lost Its Perfection

Genesis 3 tells the tragic story of humanity's fall from grace. When Adam and Eve disobeyed God's command, they broke their relationship with Him. They chose to trust their own wisdom over God's and, in doing so, sin entered the world, marring the image of God in us.

As **Psalm 51:5** states, we were all born into this sinful nature. **Romans 5:12-19** explains that sin and death spread to all humanity through Adam, and we now share in this fallen condition. Humanity's disobedience led to suffering, death, and spiritual separation from God. Sin taints our hearts, and the Apostle Paul vividly describes this inner conflict in **Romans 7:15-18**—the desire to do good but being unable to carry it out due to the power of sin within us. Our minds and hearts have been distorted by sin, and this fallen nature is passed down to each generation.

3. The Human Dilemma: The Need for Redemption

In the midst of this brokenness, we face a dilemma. We were created for something greater—something more glorious. We were made to reflect God's image and to live in harmony with Him. But sin has distorted this purpose.

Jeremiah 17:9 tells us that "the heart is deceitful above all things." Our best efforts to restore ourselves fall short. **Isaiah 64:6** reminds us that "all our righteousness are like filthy rags." No matter how hard we try, we cannot fix ourselves. Humanity's need for redemption is profound.

4. Redemption in Christ: Restoring the Image of God

But God, in His infinite love and mercy, did not leave us in our fallen state. He provided the answer through **Jesus Christ**, who came to restore what was lost. **John 3:16** reveals God's heart: "For God so loved the world that He gave His only Son, that whoever believes in Him should not perish but have eternal life."

Through Jesus' life, death, and resurrection, He took upon Himself the punishment we deserve and made a way for us to be reconciled to God. **2 Corinthians 5:21** states that "For our sake, He made Him to be sin who knew no sin, so that in Him we might become the righteousness of God." Jesus, the perfect image of God, was lifted up on the cross to redeem us and restore the image of God in us.

John 12:32 says that Jesus, when lifted up, will draw all people to Himself. His sacrifice is not only the remedy for sin, but it is also the means by which we are reconciled to God, allowing the image of God to be restored in us through the work of the Holy Spirit.

5. The Call to Choose: Living in God's Image

Just as Adam and Eve had the freedom to choose in the Garden of Eden, we too are faced with a choice today. The difference is that through **Jesus Christ**, we now have the power to choose rightly. We no longer need to be slaves to sin, for Christ has made a way for us to be free.

The Gospel calls us to live out the image of God once again. **Matthew 22:37-39** calls us to love God with all our heart, soul, and mind, and to love our neighbor as ourselves. This is the way to live as God intended—reflecting His image and fulfilling the purpose for which we were created.

6. Gospel Connection: Grace, Redemption, and Transformation

The Gospel is the good news of grace. **Ephesians 2:8-9** tells us that salvation is by grace through faith, not by our works. It is a gift from God. Through Jesus, we are offered forgiveness, healing, and restoration. The power of the Holy Spirit enables us to live transformed lives, living according to the image of Christ.

Romans 8:9-11 reminds us that the same Spirit that raised Jesus from the dead now lives in us, empowering us to live as Christ lived, fulfilling the image of God in us.

7. Application: Transformation in Jesus Christ

The Great Controversy continues today. We still face a battle between good and evil, between following Christ or yielding to sin. The choices we make matter. Every day, we can choose to live according to the image of God or to give in to the sinful nature.

But there is hope. **Philippians 2:5-11** tells us that we are to have the mind of Christ, living in humility and obedience to God. This is the way to experience true freedom and transformation. Through the Holy Spirit, God empowers us to live out this new life, reflecting His image to the world around us.

8. Appeal: Call to Transformation in Jesus

The cross of Christ is not just an event in history; it is the call to transform our lives today. Jesus was lifted up on the cross, drawing all people to Himself. The cross is where sin was defeated, and where God's restoration began.

As we reflect on our true nature—created in God's image but marred by sin—we are invited to choose transformation through Jesus. The image of God, once marred by sin, is being restored through His sacrifice.

Invitation: I invite you today to lift Jesus up in your life, to choose Him as your Savior, and to allow His Holy Spirit to restore you to the image of your Creator. Jesus is drawing you to Himself. Will you respond to His call?

Key Statement to Conclude the Sermon: "The cross is not just an event in history; it is the call to transform your life today. Lift up Jesus, and let Him draw you to Himself."

Will you choose Jesus today and allow Him to restore His image in you?

Sermon 5

"The Great Controversy and Looking to Jesus as our Victory"

Revelation 12:7-9, Ephesians 6:12, Genesis 3:1-5

In every captivating story, there are clear heroes and villains. The battle between good and evil is starkly drawn, and we instinctively find ourselves rooting for the hero. In the world around us, however, the lines between good and evil can appear blurred. We witness acts of heroism mixed with imperfection, and individuals striving for good who sometimes fail or falter.

This confusion is not new, and the Bible helps us understand why: we are living in a battle—a battle not of flesh and blood but of spiritual significance. This is the Great Controversy, the ongoing cosmic war between God and Satan, a war for the character of God, His law, and His sovereignty. And we, human beings, are caught right in the middle.

I. The Battle's Beginning: Rebellion in Heaven

Before the earth even existed, the battle began in heaven. Lucifer, the "Morning Star," was once one of God's most glorious angels, a being of immense beauty and wisdom. Ezekiel 28:12-15 paints a picture of his perfection. Yet, pride crept into his heart. He began to question why, with all his brilliance, he was not equal to God. The first sin was born not of external action but internal pride.

Isaiah 14:13-14 tells us that Lucifer desired to ascend to God's throne, seeking self-exaltation, and thereby became the adversary, Satan. A rebellion followed, and Lucifer led a third of the angels into mutiny. This rebellion was not against a mere earthly king but against the Sovereign of the universe, and it resulted in war in heaven.

Revelation 12:7-9 recounts this war: "Now war arose in heaven, Michael and his angels fighting against the dragon. And the dragon and his angels fought back, but he was defeated..." Satan and his angels were cast out of heaven, and the earth became the battleground where the cosmic conflict would continue.

II. The Battle Comes to Earth: The Fall of Humanity

When Satan was cast out of heaven, he did not retreat into obscurity. Instead, he targeted humanity, God's new creation. He approached Eve in the Garden of Eden, seeking to corrupt God's perfect world. In Genesis 3:1-5, Satan questioned God's character, asking, "Did God actually say...?" He introduced doubt, suggesting that God was withholding something good from Eve, leading her to believe that by disobeying, she would become like God.

Eve, intrigued and deceived, took the fruit and ate it, and Adam followed. With this act, humanity took sides in the rebellion. The knowledge of good and evil entered the world, and the perfect relationship between humanity and God was shattered. The consequences of that choice were dire—sin entered the world, and with it, death and suffering.

III. Our Role in the Battle: Choosing Sides

We may wonder, "How does this ancient battle affect me today?" The answer is simple: we are still in the midst of it. Every day, we make choices—choices that reflect whether we will align ourselves with God's love or Satan's lies. Ephesians 6:12 reminds us that our struggle is not against flesh and blood but against spiritual forces of evil in the heavenly realms.

Satan still seeks to deceive, to sow doubt about God's goodness, and to lure us into rebellion. But God has given us the power to resist. James 4:7-8 tells us, "Submit to God. Resist the devil, and he will flee from you." We are not alone in this battle. Jesus Christ, our Savior, has already secured the ultimate victory.

IV. God's Ultimate Victory: A New Heaven and Earth

We may feel overwhelmed at times by the struggles we face in this world, but we know how this battle ends. Revelation 20 speaks of the final defeat of Satan and his followers, and a new heaven and earth where God will dwell with His people. The victory has been won on the cross, where Jesus defeated sin and death once and for all.

In John 3:16-17, we are reminded that "God so loved the world that He gave His only Son, that whoever believes in Him should not perish but have eternal life." Jesus' sacrifice was the decisive blow to Satan's power, and His resurrection ensures that those who trust in Him will share in His victory.

V. Living in Victory: The Promise of Hope

Even as we wait for the final victory, we can live in the hope that Christ has already conquered. Matthew 11:28-30 offers us rest from the burden of sin: "Come to me, all who are weary and burdened, and I will give you rest." We do not fight this battle alone. The Holy Spirit empowers us, and God's promises guide us.

In this Great Controversy, we are called to make daily choices that reflect our allegiance to God. The decisions we make matter, not just for ourselves but for the entire universe, which watches our lives unfold. Our witness to the world is part of the story of God's ultimate vindication.

Conclusion: Choose Whose Side You Are On

Today, the battle continues, but we know the outcome. Christ has won the victory, and we are called to stand firm in Him. As we navigate the confusion and struggles of life, let us hold fast to His promises. Choose His side, and remember that "we are more than conquerors through Him who loved us" (Romans 8:37).

In the end, the Great Controversy will conclude with the return of Christ, the destruction of evil, and the restoration of all things. Until then, may we choose daily to fight the good fight, standing firm in the victory already won for us by Jesus Christ. Amen.

Sermon 6

"The Life, Death, and Resurrection of Jesus Christ"

1. Introduction: The Heart of the Story - Attention Grabber: In the story of humanity, we see the darkness of sin clouding the world, a separation from the God who created us. Romans 3:23 tells us, "all have sinned and fall short of the glory of God."

- Transition to Biblical Passage:
  Despite the weight of our sin, there is an incredible truth we must never forget: God is love (1 John 4:8). This love compelled God to devise a plan before the foundation of the world (Ephesians 1:3-14) to redeem

humanity.

Jesus Christ—His only Son—entered the world to live among us and ultimately sacrifice Himself for our sins.

2. Jesus: Fully God and Fully Man

- The Mystery of the Incarnation:
  Let us first marvel at the mystery of the incarnation. Jesus, the eternal Word, became flesh and dwelt among us (John 1:14).
- The Dual Nature of Christ:
  Though He is fully God, He chose to take on our humanity.
  Born in humble circumstances, in a stable, with no royal welcome except from a few shepherds (Luke 2:7-20).
  Philippians 2:6-8 explains that Jesus did not cling to His divine privileges but emptied Himself, becoming a servant.
- Jesus' Perfect Life:
  Jesus lived the perfect life that humanity failed to live. His innocent blood is the only sacrifice that could cover our sins.

3. Jesus' Ministry: A Life of Love and Healing

- Demonstration of God's Love:
  As Jesus began His public ministry, He demonstrated God's love by healing the sick, giving sight to the

blind, making the lame walk, and raising the dead (Matthew 20:30-34, Luke 7:11-17).

- Jesus' Compassion:
  He spent time with the outcasts of society, shared the good news with the poor (Luke 4:18), and taught people to love one another as He had loved them (John 13:34-35).
  He was not concerned with wealth or status but with serving others.

4. The Cross: Jesus' Ultimate Sacrifice for Our Sins

- The Greatest Demonstration of Love:
  The greatest demonstration of God's love was the sacrifice of Jesus on the cross.
  Jesus knew the price He had to pay for our sins, and He willingly laid down His life for us.
  John 15:13 says, "Greater love has no one than this, that someone lay down his life for his friends."

- Jesus' Death as Substitutionary:
  Jesus' death was not just an example of love, but the ultimate sacrifice—the perfect atonement for our sins.
  1 Peter 1:18-19 reminds us that we were redeemed not with perishable things like silver or gold, but with the precious blood of Christ.

- The Penalty of Sin:
  At the cross, Jesus bore the penalty of sin that we deserved.
  His death was substitutionary—He died in our place.

His blood satisfies the justice of God and offers forgiveness for all who believe in Him.

5. The Resurrection: Triumph Over Death

- Victory Over Death:
  Jesus did not remain in the grave. He rose again on the third day, conquering death and the power of sin (1 Corinthians 15:20-22).
- Eternal Life in Christ:
  The resurrection is not just a historical event; it is the declaration that Jesus has triumphed over the forces of evil.
  All who accept His sacrifice will share in His victory. Romans 6:4 says, "We were therefore buried with Him through baptism into death...just as Christ was raised from the dead, we too may live a new life."
- Hope Through His Resurrection:
  Through His resurrection, Jesus opened the door for eternal life, offering us the hope of victory over sin and death.

6. Jesus' Love for Us: A Call to Respond

- The Call to Respond:
  The life, death, and resurrection of Jesus Christ reveal to us the infinite and holy love of the Creator.
  This love led Jesus to leave His throne in heaven, to live a humble life, and to die a criminal's death for our sake.

- The Challenge:
  It is a love that calls us to respond.
  How are we responding to His sacrifice? Are we living in the freedom that He has provided? Are we sharing His love with others as He shared it with us?

7. Conclusion: The Foundation of Our Faith

- Restoring Our Relationship with God:
  Jesus' life, death, and resurrection are the foundation of our faith.
  In Him, we see the perfect love of God—love that humbled itself, love that served, and love that sacrificed for us.
- Hope of Eternal Life:
  Because of Jesus, we can have a restored relationship with God, and we can look forward to eternal life with Him.
  Let us embrace this love, live in the power of His resurrection, and share His love with a world that desperately needs it.

8. Invitation: Open Your Heart to Jesus

- Personal Invitation:
  If you have not yet experienced the love of Christ in your life, I invite you to open your heart to Him today. He died for you. He rose again for you.

Will you accept His invitation to be part of His eternal kingdom?

Sermon Summary:
This sermon highlights the life, death, and resurrection of Jesus Christ, focusing on His role as both fully God and fully man. It emphasizes Jesus' ministry of love and healing, His ultimate sacrifice on the cross, and His triumph over death through the resurrection. The sermon invites listeners to respond to God's infinite love and to live in the power of His resurrection.

Sermon 7

""The Experience of Salvation"

Text: John 12:32 – "And I, if I be lifted up from the earth, will draw all men unto me."

1. Introduction

- **Grab the Attention:**
    - Imagine standing at the edge of a cliff, with nothing but the vastness of the unknown before you. You're stuck, uncertain, and

afraid. Then someone extends a hand, and in that moment, you realize that help is here.
  - The story of salvation is like that extended hand — God offering to lift us from the brink of destruction. In John 12:32, Jesus offers Himself as that hand, lifting us up from the pit of sin and despair.
- **Transition into the Biblical Passage:**
  - Today, we will explore what it truly means to experience salvation — to be lifted up by Jesus Christ, who draws us to Himself through His life, death, and resurrection.
- **Read John 12:32** with Passion:
  - "And I, if I be lifted up from the earth, will draw all men unto me."
  - This is Jesus speaking of His sacrifice, the act of lifting Him up on the cross, which would draw all people to Him.

2. The Problem: The Sinful Condition of Humanity

- **What is the Biblical Problem?**
  - Humanity, in its sin, is separated from God. Romans 3:23 declares, "For all have sinned and fall short of the glory of God."
  - In this condition, we are alienated from God, facing eternal death as the wages of sin. We are stuck in the brokenness of the Great Controversy, a battle between Christ and Satan, where sin has caused deep division and destruction (1 Peter 5:8, Revelation 12:4-9).
- **Humanity's Need for a Savior:**

- - Our disobedience, like Adam and Eve's in the Garden, has created this chasm between us and God. We are powerless to overcome this separation on our own, and the law demands justice (Romans 6:23).
  - **Connect to the Great Controversy:**
    - Satan seeks to devour, deceive, and destroy us, but God is calling us back into His embrace. The very struggle of the ages, the Great Controversy, is about who we will follow — Christ or Satan. The enemy works tirelessly to keep us bound in sin, but Christ offers the way out.
  - **Transition Statement to the Biblical Solution:**
    - But there is hope. Jesus, who was lifted up on the cross, is the solution to our problem. Through His sacrifice, He draws us to Himself, offering salvation and victory.

3. The Solution: Jesus Christ, Our Savior

- **What Does the Text Say About God?**
  - John 12:32 shows us that God's plan was always to draw humanity to Himself through Jesus. Jesus' death was not just a tragedy; it was the means of our salvation.
- **Expound on the Victory in Jesus:**
  - Through Jesus' life, death, and resurrection, God provides the ultimate solution. Romans 5:8 says, "But God demonstrates His own love toward us, in that while we were still sinners, Christ died for us." His death on the cross satisfies the demands of God's law, and His resurrection ensures our eternal life.

- **Lift Up Jesus:**
    - Jesus was lifted up on the cross, not just physically but as the Savior of the world, drawing us to Himself. This is the ultimate demonstration of God's love — that He gave His Son for sinners like you and me (John 3:16, Acts 4:12).

4. Main Point: "Lifted Up, Drawn In"

- **Key Phrase:**
    - "Lifted Up, Drawn In" — Jesus' sacrifice draws us to Him, offering salvation, redemption, and eternal life.
    - This phrase encapsulates the experience of salvation: Jesus is lifted up, and we are drawn to Him, receiving the gift of life.

5. Gospel Connection: God's Grace and Redemption

- **Connect the Main Point to the Gospel:**
    - The Good News is that through Jesus' death and resurrection, we can be reconciled with God, made new, and assured of eternal life.
    - God's love is unshakable. Ephesians 2:8-9 reminds us, "For by grace you have been saved through faith, and that not of yourselves; it is the gift of God."
- **The Transformation in Christ:**
    - Through the Holy Spirit, we are transformed. Jesus' life, death, and resurrection are not just historical facts but the means through which we are made new (Romans 12:2, 2 Corinthians 5:17).

6. Application: The Transformative Power of Salvation

- **Apply the Biblical Problem to Our Current Situation:**
    - The battle between good and evil is still at work in our lives today. We face temptations, struggles, and doubts. But Jesus offers us victory. We do not need to be enslaved by sin or fear. Through His Spirit, we are empowered to live differently.
- **Apply the Main Point to the Audience:**
    - Just as Jesus was lifted up, we too are called to be lifted up in Him. When we believe in Jesus, we are drawn into His love and grace. This changes everything about who we are and how we live.
- **Preach Gospel Hope:**
    - Jesus is inviting you today to experience this salvation. In Him, you find forgiveness, hope, and eternal life. You no longer need to fear the consequences of sin because Jesus has already won the victory (Philippians 2:5-11).

7. Appeal: Call for Transformation in Jesus

- **Key Statement to Conclude:**
    - "Lifted up, drawn in." Jesus has been lifted up on the cross to draw you to Himself. Will you accept His invitation today?
- **Invitation:**
    - Jesus is calling you. Will you experience His salvation today? Will you accept the gift of eternal life and allow the Holy Spirit to transform your heart and mind? Jesus offers

this to you now. Respond to His call, and let Him lift you up from the depths of sin into His glorious light.

Final Prayer:

- Heavenly Father, thank You for the incredible gift of salvation through Jesus Christ. We lift Him up in our hearts and minds today, recognizing His sacrifice for our sins. May His love draw us closer to Him, and may His Holy Spirit transform us, empowering us to live for Him. In Jesus' name, Amen.

Sermon 8

*""The Experience of Salvation"

Text: John 12:32 - "And I, if I be lifted up from the earth, will draw all men unto me."

Opening Scripture: 2 Corinthians 5:17-21 - "In Christ, we are a new creation; the old has gone, the new is here."

- **Main Theme**: Salvation is a transformative experience encompassing past, present, and future dimensions, initiated and sustained by God's love through Christ.
- **Purpose**: To inspire and challenge believers to embrace and live out the full experience of salvation.

I. Salvation in the Past: God's Act of Redemption

1. **Key Point**: Salvation begins with God's initiative of grace.
    - **Scripture**: 2 Corinthians 5:21 – Christ became sin for us so we might become righteous.
    - **Illustration**: The prisoner on death row pardoned at the last moment (John 3:16; Acts 4:12).
2. **Aspects of Salvation:**
    - **Repentance**: Acknowledging sin and turning to God (Acts 2:37-38).
    - **Confession**: David's heartfelt prayer in Psalm 51:3-10.
    - **Forgiveness and Justification**: God's pardon is not earned but given freely (Romans 5:6-10).

II. Salvation in the Present: Transformation Through Christ

1. **Key Point**: Salvation is an ongoing work of sanctification by the Holy Spirit.
    - **Scripture**: 2 Corinthians 3:18 – Being transformed into Christ's likeness.
    - **Illustration**: A sculptor chiseling away imperfections to reveal the masterpiece.
2. **Work of the Spirit: Renewing the Mind**: Romans 12:2 – Transformation begins with the renewal of the mind.
    - **Empowering Holy Living**: Ezekiel 36:25-27 – God gives a new heart and spirit.

- **Abiding in Christ**: John 15:4-5 – The source of spiritual fruitfulness.

III. Salvation in the Future: The Hope of Eternal Glory

1. **Key Point**: Salvation culminates in eternal life with Christ.
   - **Scripture**: Titus 3:3-7 – The hope of eternal life through God's mercy.
   - **Illustration**: The bride being presented in splendor (Ephesians 5:25-27).
2. **Future Assurance**:
   - **Adopted as God's Children**: Romans 8:14-17 – We are heirs with Christ.
   - **Partakers of the Divine Nature**: 2 Peter 1:3-4 – Sharing in God's eternal glory.

IV. Living the Experience of Salvation

1. **Restfulness in Christ**:
   - **Scripture**: Matthew 11:28-30 – Jesus offers rest for our souls.
   - **Encouragement**: Salvation is not about striving but abiding in Christ's love.
2. **Daily Transformation**:
   - **Focus on Christ**: Contemplate His love, purity, and self-denial.
   - **Practical Application**: Depend wholly on Him for strength, wisdom, and holiness.

Conclusion

- **Challenge**: Are you embracing the full experience of salvation – past forgiveness, present transformation, and future hope?
- **Call to Action**:
    - Surrender completely to Christ and allow His Spirit to transform your life.
    - Share the hope and joy of salvation with others.
- **Closing Scripture**: John 14:6 – Jesus is the way, the truth, and the life.

Final Prayer

- Thank God for His infinite love and mercy in providing salvation through Christ.
- Ask for the Holy Spirit's guidance in living a holy life and growing in Christlikeness.
- Commit to sharing the transformative power of salvation with others.

Sermon 9

The Church

Text: Matthew 16:18 - "And I tell you that you are Peter, and on this rock I will build my church, and the gates of Hades will not overcome it."

1. Introduction:

- **Grab Attention:** The Church is not just a building; it's a living body of believers united in Christ.
- **Transition into Passage:** Let's explore how Jesus envisioned His Church and what that means for us today.

2. Problem:

- **Biblical Problem:** The world is divided, and humanity is lost in sin. (Romans 3:23)
- **Great Controversy Connection:** Satan seeks to destroy the Church, but Christ will protect it.

3. Solution:

- **Biblical Solution:** Jesus is the foundation of the Church, and through Him, we are called to be His ambassadors in the world.
- **Connect to Jesus:** Jesus died to establish the Church, empowering it with the Holy Spirit to carry out His mission.

4. Main Point: "The Church is the body of Christ, called to fulfill His mission."

5. Gospel Connection: The Church is Christ's instrument for salvation, and through it, the message of redemption reaches the world.

6. Application: The Church isn't a building; it's the people of God. As members, we are called to work together to bring others to Jesus.

7. Appeal: Will you be part of the Church that Jesus built, fulfilling His mission on earth?

Sermon 10

The Remnant and its Mission

Text: Revelation 12:17 – "Then the dragon was enraged at the woman and went off to make war against the rest of her offspring—those who keep God's commands and hold fast their testimony about Jesus."

1. Introduction:

- **Grab Attention:** God always has a faithful remnant who stand for truth.

- **Transition into Passage:** What does it mean to be part of God's remnant today?

2. Problem:

- **Biblical Problem:** The remnant faces opposition from the enemy.
- **Great Controversy Connection:** The battle between Christ and Satan is waged against the remnant.

3. Solution:

- **Biblical Solution:** Jesus calls the remnant to stand firm in faith, keeping His commandments and testimony.
- **Connect to Jesus:** Jesus is the center of the remnant's message.

4. Main Point: "The remnant's mission is to proclaim the everlasting gospel."

5. Gospel Connection: As the remnant, we are called to share the good news of salvation and to live out the truths of God's Word.

6. Application: Will you stand as part of God's remnant, proclaiming His love and truth to a lost world?

7. Appeal: Accept Christ's call to be part of His remnant and join the mission of spreading His gospel.

Sermon 11

Unity in the Body of Christ

Text: **1 Corinthians 12:12-13** – "Just as a body, though one, has many parts, but all its many parts form one body, so it is with Christ."

1. Introduction:

- **Grab Attention:** In Christ, we are united despite our differences.
- **Transition into Passage:** Let's explore how unity in the body of Christ reflects Christ's love for us.

2. Problem:

- **Biblical Problem:** Disunity causes division and hinders the gospel.
- **Great Controversy Connection:** Satan works to sow discord, but Christ's love unites.

3. Solution:

- **Biblical Solution:** Unity is found in Christ, who binds us together as one body.
- **Connect to Jesus:** Through Christ, the Church is united despite differences.

4. Main Point: "Unity in the body of Christ reflects the unity of the Trinity."

5. Gospel Connection: Christ's death and resurrection made unity possible. Through His love, we are called to love one another.

6. Application: Embrace the call for unity within the body of Christ by showing love, understanding, and service to one another.

7. Appeal: Will you commit to unity in the body of Christ, reflecting His love to the world?

Sermon 12

Baptism

Text: Matthew 28:19 – "Therefore go and make disciples of all nations, baptizing them in the name of the Father and of the Son and of the Holy Spirit."

1. Introduction:

- **Grab Attention:** Baptism is more than a ritual; it's a public declaration of faith in Jesus.
- **Transition into Passage:** Let's explore the significance of baptism in the life of a believer.

2. **Problem:**

    - **Biblical Problem:** Sin separates us from God, and baptism symbolizes the cleansing and renewal Jesus offers.
    - **Great Controversy Connection:** Baptism is a mark of allegiance to Christ in the midst of the battle between good and evil.

3. **Solution:**

    - **Biblical Solution:** Baptism is a sign of our identification with Jesus in His death, burial, and resurrection.
    - **Connect to Jesus:** Jesus Himself was baptized to fulfill all righteousness, and He calls us to do the same.

4. **Main Point:** "Baptism is the outward symbol of an inward transformation through Jesus."

5. **Gospel Connection:** In baptism, we participate in the death and resurrection of Christ, symbolizing our new life in Him.

6. **Application:** If you haven't yet been baptized, consider making this declaration of faith today. If you have been baptized, live out the transformation it symbolizes.

7. Appeal: If you haven't been baptized, will you take this step of faith today? Will you renew your commitment to live for Christ?

Sermon 13

The Lord's Supper

Text: 1 Corinthians 11:23-24 – "For I received from the Lord what I also passed on to you: The Lord Jesus, on the night he was betrayed, took bread, and when he had given thanks, he broke it and said, 'This is my body, which is for you; do this in remembrance of me.'"

1. **Introduction:**
   - **Grab Attention:** The Lord's Supper is a sacred moment to remember Christ's sacrifice.
   - **Transition into Passage:** Let's understand the significance of this ordinance in our walk with Jesus.

2. **Problem:**
   - **Biblical Problem:** We often forget the price of our salvation and take Christ's sacrifice for granted.
   - **Great Controversy Connection:** The Lord's Supper reminds us of Christ's victory over Satan and the power of the cross.

3. **Solution:**
   - **Biblical Solution:** The Lord's Supper is an invitation to remember Christ's sacrifice and renew our covenant with Him.
   - **Connect to Jesus:** Jesus' body and blood, broken and shed for us, offer forgiveness and eternal life.

4. **Main Point:** "The Lord's Supper calls us to remember Christ's sacrifice and live in His grace."

5. **Gospel Connection:** The Lord's Supper is a reminder that through Jesus' body and blood, we are forgiven and transformed.

6. **Application:** Let the Lord's Supper be a time to reflect on Jesus' sacrifice and renew your commitment to Him.

7. **Appeal:** Will you take this time to remember Jesus' sacrifice and recommit your life to Him?

Sermon 14

Spiritual Gifts and Ministries

Text: **1 Corinthians 12:4-7** – "There are different kinds of gifts, but the same Spirit distributes them. There are different kinds of service, but the same Lord."

1. Introduction:

- **Grab Attention:** Every believer has a unique role in the body of Christ.
- **Transition into Passage:** Let's discover how spiritual gifts empower us for service in God's kingdom.

2. Problem:

- **Biblical Problem:** The Church is ineffective when members neglect their spiritual gifts.
- **Great Controversy Connection:** Satan seeks to divide and discourage, but the Holy Spirit unites and empowers us.

3. Solution:

- **Biblical Solution:** The Holy Spirit equips each believer with spiritual gifts for ministry.
- **Connect to Jesus:** Jesus has given us the Holy Spirit to empower us for service in His name.

4. Main Point: "Each believer is gifted by the Spirit for ministry in the body of Christ."

5. Gospel Connection: Through the Holy Spirit, Christ equips us to serve and build His kingdom.

6. Application: Discover your spiritual gifts and use them to serve others in the body of Christ.

7. Appeal: Will you commit to using your spiritual gifts for the glory of God and the advancement of His kingdom?

Sermon 15

The Gift of Prophecy

Text: Revelation 19:10 – "For the testimony of Jesus is the spirit of prophecy."

1. Introduction: Grab Attention: Prophecy is not just about predicting the future; it's about revealing God's will to guide and prepare us for what's ahead.

> **Transition into Passage:** Let's understand how the gift of prophecy helps us grow in our relationship with God.

2. Problem: The world is filled with confusion, and we need divine guidance.

- **Great Controversy Connection:** In the last days, God gives His prophetic voice to warn and prepare His people.

3. Solution:

- **Biblical Solution:** The gift of prophecy is God's way of speaking to His people, providing direction and correction.
- **Connect to Jesus:** The spirit of prophecy points us to Jesus and leads us closer to Him.

4. Main Point: "The gift of prophecy guides us into all truth and prepares us for Christ's return."

5. Gospel Connection: Through the gift of prophecy, God reveals His love and guidance, pointing us to salvation in Jesus.

6. Application: Embrace the messages of prophecy in Scripture and the modern-day prophet, Ellen White, as a source of wisdom and direction.

7. Appeal: Will you open your heart to the prophetic guidance God offers to lead you closer to Christ?

Sermon 16

The Law of God

Text: 1 John 5:3 – "In fact, this is love for God: to keep his commands. And his commands are not burdensome."

1. Introduction: Grab Attention: God's law is a reflection of His character—holy, loving, and perfect.

- **Transition into Passage:** Let's explore how God's law reveals His will and invites us to live in harmony with Him.

2. Problem: Sin leads to brokenness and separation from God, and His law reveals the way to restoration.

- **Great Controversy Connection:** The law is central to the conflict between Christ and Satan; it's a standard of truth and righteousness.

3. Solution: God's law is not a burden but a guide that leads to freedom and peace in Christ.

- **Connect to Jesus:** Jesus fulfilled the law perfectly, showing us how to live in obedience to God's will.

4. Main Point: "The Law of God is a reflection of His love and a guide to a life of holiness."

5. Gospel Connection: The law points to Jesus, who enables us to fulfill it through the power of the Holy Spirit.

6. Application: Embrace God's law as a guide to living in Christ's likeness, not out of obligation, but out of love for Him.

7. Appeal: Will you commit to living in harmony with God's law, allowing His love to transform your life?

Sermon 17

The Sabbath

Text: Exodus 20:8-10 – "Remember the Sabbath day by keeping it holy. Six days you shall labor and do all your work, but the seventh day is a Sabbath to the Lord your God."

1. Introduction:

- **Grab Attention:** The Sabbath is a gift from God—a time to rest and reconnect with our Creator.
- **Transition into Passage:** Let's explore why the Sabbath is so special and how it points us to Jesus.

2. Problem:

- **Biblical Problem:** We live in a busy, stressful world, and it's easy to neglect our need for rest and spiritual renewal.
- **Great Controversy Connection:** The Sabbath is a sign of loyalty to God in the great controversy between good and evil.

3. Solution:

- **Biblical Solution:** The Sabbath is a day of rest and worship, a time to recharge physically, mentally, and spiritually.
- **Connect to Jesus:** Jesus, as Lord of the Sabbath, invites us to find rest in Him and experience the fullness of life He offers.

4. Main Point: "The Sabbath is a weekly reminder of God's grace and our need for rest in Him."

5. Gospel Connection: The Sabbath points us to the rest we find in Christ, who offers peace for our souls.

6. Application: Set aside the Sabbath as a holy time to rest in God's presence and reflect on His love and goodness.

7. Appeal: Will you embrace the Sabbath as a time to rest and be refreshed in your relationship with Jesus?

Sermon 18

Stewardship

Text: 1 Corinthians 4:2 – "Now it is required that those who have been given a trust must prove faithful."

1. Introduction:

- **Grab Attention:** God has entrusted us with everything we have—our time, talents, and resources.
- **Transition into Passage:** Let's discover how we can be faithful stewards of the gifts God has given us.

2. Problem:

- **Biblical Problem:** We often become focused on our own needs and desires, forgetting that everything belongs to God.
- **Great Controversy Connection:** Stewardship is part of the battle for the ownership of our hearts and lives between God and Satan.

3. **Solution:**

- **Biblical Solution:** Stewardship is about managing God's resources with faithfulness, generosity, and accountability.
- **Connect to Jesus:** Jesus modeled perfect stewardship, using His time and resources to serve others and glorify God.

4. **Main Point:** "Stewardship is our response to God's love, faithfully managing His gifts for His glory."

5. **Gospel Connection:** Jesus, as the ultimate steward, gave His life for us, and He calls us to live lives of faithful service in return.

6. **Application:** Evaluate your life and determine how you can be a better steward of your time, talents, and resources for God's kingdom.

7. **Appeal:** Will you commit to being a faithful steward, using all that you have for God's glory and the good of others?

Sermon 19

Christian Behavior

Text: Philippians 1:27 – "Whatever happens, conduct yourselves in a manner worthy of the gospel of Christ."

1. Introduction:

- **Grab Attention:** Our behavior should reflect the transformation Christ has made in our lives.
- **Transition into Passage:** Let's explore what it means to live a life that honors Jesus in every aspect.

2. Problem:

- **Biblical Problem:** The world's values often conflict with the principles of Christ, and we struggle to live up to His calling.
- **Great Controversy Connection:** Our behavior is a testimony in the ongoing battle between good and evil.

3. Solution:

- **Biblical Solution:** Christ calls us to live a life that reflects His character—humble, loving, and obedient.
- **Connect to Jesus:** Jesus lived a perfect life, showing us how to live according to God's will.

4. Main Point: "Christian behavior is a reflection of Christ's character in us, demonstrating His love to the world."

5. Gospel Connection: Through the power of the Holy Spirit, we are empowered to live Christlike lives, bearing witness to His transformative grace.

6. Application: Examine your behavior and ask, "Am I living in a way that honors Christ and reflects His love?"

7. Appeal: Will you commit to living in a manner worthy of the gospel, allowing Christ to transform your behavior for His glory?

Sermon 20

Marriage and the Family

Text: Ephesians 5:31-32 – "For this reason a man shall leave his father and mother and be joined to his wife, and the two shall become one flesh. This is a great mystery, but I speak concerning Christ and the church."

1. Introduction:

- **Grab Attention:** Marriage is more than a relationship between two people—it's a reflection of the relationship between Christ and His church.
- **Transition into Passage:** Let's explore how marriage and family are central to God's plan and how they point to Jesus.

2. Problem:

- **Biblical Problem:** Marriage and family have been distorted by sin, leading to brokenness, pain, and confusion.
- **Great Controversy Connection:** The family is central to God's kingdom, and Satan seeks to destroy it as part of his attack on God's creation.

3. Solution:

- **Biblical Solution:** Christ restores the relationship between husband and wife, teaching us self-sacrificial love.
- **Connect to Jesus:** Jesus' love for the church sets the example for sacrificial love in marriage. He is the one who brings healing to broken relationships.

4. Main Point: "Marriage and family are a reflection of Christ's love for His church, and through Him, we can restore and reflect this love."

5. Gospel Connection: Through Christ's sacrifice, we learn to love one another in our marriages and families, reflecting His love for us.

6. Application: Strengthen your marriage and family by placing Christ at the center, allowing His love to transform your relationships.

7. Appeal: Will you invite Jesus into your marriage and family, allowing His love to restore and strengthen your relationships?

Sermon 21

Christ's Ministry in the Heavenly Sanctuary

Text: Hebrews 8:1-2 – "Now of the things which we have spoken this is the sum: We have such a high priest, who is set on the right hand of the throne of the Majesty in the heavens; a minister of the sanctuary, and of the true tabernacle, which the Lord pitched, and not man."

1. Introduction:

- **Grab Attention:** Christ's work as our High Priest in the heavenly sanctuary is vital to our salvation and our understanding of His role today.
- **Transition into Passage:** Let's discover how Jesus' ministry in the sanctuary impacts our daily lives and draws us nearer to God.

2. Problem:

- **Biblical Problem:** Humanity is separated from God due to sin, and we need an intercessor to restore our relationship with Him.
- **Great Controversy Connection:** The sanctuary service is part of the cosmic battle between good and evil, where Christ intercedes for us.

3. Solution:

- **Biblical Solution:** Jesus, our High Priest, intercedes on our behalf, making atonement for our sins and securing our salvation.
- **Connect to Jesus:** Through His ministry in the heavenly sanctuary, Jesus continues His work of redemption, bringing us into the presence of God.

4. Main Point: "Christ's ministry in the heavenly sanctuary guarantees our salvation and draws us into intimate relationship with God."

5. Gospel Connection: Jesus' intercessory work is a continuous demonstration of His love and grace, providing us with ongoing forgiveness and spiritual renewal.

6. Application: Trust in Christ's work as your High Priest, knowing that He is interceding on your behalf every moment.

7. Appeal: Will you accept Jesus as your High Priest, allowing His ongoing ministry in the sanctuary to transform your life?

Sermon 22

The Second Coming of Christ

Text: Revelation 22:12 – "Behold, I am coming quickly, and My reward is with Me, to give to every one according to his work."

1. Introduction:

- **Grab Attention:** The return of Jesus is the most anticipated event in Christian history, bringing ultimate hope to all believers.
- **Transition into Passage:** Let's explore what the Second Coming means for us today and how we can live in eager expectation.

2. **Problem:**

- **Biblical Problem:** The world is filled with suffering, pain, and injustice, and we long for Jesus to return and make things right.
- **Great Controversy Connection:** The Second Coming marks the end of Satan's rule and the ultimate victory of Christ over evil.

3. **Solution:**

- **Biblical Solution:** Jesus' return will bring justice, peace, and the full realization of God's kingdom on earth.
- **Connect to Jesus:** The Second Coming is the culmination of Christ's redemptive work, bringing us into eternal fellowship with Him.

4. **Main Point:** "The Second Coming of Christ is the ultimate fulfillment of God's promise to restore all things and bring justice to the world."

5. Gospel Connection: The return of Jesus is the final act of God's love and redemption, bringing to completion the salvation He began on the cross.

6. Application: Live with the hope and anticipation of Christ's return, letting that hope shape the way you live today.

7. Appeal: Will you live in readiness for the return of Jesus, eagerly awaiting His coming and preparing your heart for His arrival?

Sermon 23

Death and Resurrection

Text: 1 Corinthians 15:20-22 – "But now Christ is risen from the dead, and has become the firstfruits of those who have fallen asleep. For since by man came death, by Man also came the resurrection of the dead. For as in Adam all die, even so in Christ all shall be made alive."

1. Introduction:

- **Grab Attention:** Death is a universal reality, but Christ's resurrection gives us hope beyond the grave.
- **Transition into Passage:** Let's dive into the hope of resurrection and what it means for us as believers in Christ.

2. Problem:

- **Biblical Problem:** Death came through sin, and humanity is bound to experience it, but death is not the end of the story.
- **Great Controversy Connection:** Death and resurrection are key events in the battle between Christ and Satan—Christ's resurrection is the victory over death.

3. Solution:

- **Biblical Solution:** Jesus, through His death and resurrection, has conquered the power of death, offering eternal life to all who believe in Him.
- **Connect to Jesus:** Christ's resurrection is the assurance that we, too, will be resurrected and live forever with Him.

4. Main Point: "Through Jesus' death and resurrection, we have the victory over death and the promise of eternal life."

5. Gospel Connection: Jesus' victory over death guarantees that all who trust in Him will also be resurrected to eternal life.

6. Application: Live with the hope of the resurrection, knowing that death is not the end but a transition to eternal life in Christ.

7. Appeal: Will you embrace the hope of resurrection in Jesus, trusting in His victory over death and its power in your life?

Sermon 24

The Millennium and the End of Sin

Text: Revelation 20:1-3 – "Then I saw an angel coming down from heaven, having the key to the bottomless pit and a great chain in his hand. He laid hold of the dragon, that serpent of old, who is the Devil and Satan, and bound him for a thousand years."

1. Introduction:

- **Grab Attention:** The Millennium is the period when sin and Satan are finally defeated, and Christ reigns with His saints.
- **Transition into Passage:** Let's explore what the Bible teaches about the Millennium and how it marks the final defeat of sin.

2. Problem:

- **Biblical Problem:** The world is marred by sin, and the battle between good and evil continues. The Millennium marks the time when God will finally eradicate sin and its consequences.
- **Great Controversy Connection:** The Millennium is the final phase of the great controversy, where God's justice and mercy are fully revealed.

3. Solution:

- **Biblical Solution:** During the Millennium, Satan is bound, and God's people reign with Christ, bringing ultimate peace and justice.
- **Connect to Jesus:** Christ's reign during the Millennium is the fulfillment of His promise to restore all things and end the reign of evil.

4. Main Point:
"The Millennium is the final phase of God's redemptive plan, bringing an end to sin and its consequences."

5. Gospel Connection: Jesus' victory over sin during the Millennium assures us of His power to redeem and restore all things.

6. Application: Live with the hope that Jesus will one day end sin and suffering and reign forever with His people.

7. Appeal: Will you place your trust in Jesus, knowing that He will one day end sin and restore His kingdom of peace and righteousness?

Sermon 25

The New Earth

Text: Revelation 21:1-4 – "Now I saw a new heaven and a new earth, for the first heaven and the first earth had passed away. Also, there was no more sea. Then I, John, saw the holy city, New Jerusalem, coming down out of heaven from God, prepared as a bride adorned for her husband."

1. Introduction:

- **Grab Attention:** The New Earth is God's final gift to His people, a place where there will be no more pain, death, or sorrow.
- **Transition into Passage:** Let's explore what the Bible says about the New Earth and the hope it brings to believers.

2. Problem:

- **Biblical Problem:** The current earth is tainted by sin, suffering, and death, and we long for the restoration of all things.
- **Great Controversy Connection:** The New Earth is the final victory of God over sin, where His people will live in harmony with Him forever.

3. Solution:

- **Biblical Solution:** God will create a new heaven and new earth, free from sin and suffering, where He will dwell with His people forever.
- **Connect to Jesus:** Jesus' victory over sin secures our place in the New Earth, where we will live in eternal peace with Him.

4. Main Point: "The New Earth is the ultimate fulfillment of God's promise to restore creation and live with His people forever."

5. Gospel Connection: Jesus' death, resurrection, and second coming make the New Earth a reality for all believers, where God's presence will dwell among us.

6. Application: Live in the hope of the New Earth, allowing the anticipation of eternal peace with God to shape how you live today.

7. Appeal: Will you embrace the hope of the New Earth, knowing that God is preparing a place for you where you will dwell with Him forever?

Sermon 26

Preaching the Three Angels Messages

Introduction Grab the Attention:
Begin with a compelling illustration: *"Imagine an angel appearing in the sky with a trumpet call, delivering a message of*

eternal significance to all nations, tribes, and tongues. How would you respond?"

- **Transition to the Biblical Passage**:
  Highlight Revelation 14:6–12, the Three Angels' Messages, as God's final call to humanity.
- **Read the Text**:
  Proclaim the passage with conviction and set the stage for a Christ-centered proclamation.

2. Problem: Humanity's Need for Salvation in the Great Controversy

- **The Biblical Problem**:
  Humanity has fallen into sin, separated from God (Romans 3:23). Disobedience and rebellion characterize the human condition (Hebrews 1:22, Titus 1:15).
- **The Cosmic Context**:
  Connect the problem to the Great Controversy (Revelation 12:4–9), where Satan seeks to deceive the world and divert worship from the Creator.
- **Humanity's Need**:
  Highlight the urgent need for a Savior who can reconcile humanity to God.

3. Solution: God's Answer in Jesus Christ

- **The First Angel's Message**:
  - Proclaim the everlasting gospel: Worship the Creator who made heaven and earth (Revelation 14:6–7).
  - Point to Jesus as the Creator and Redeemer (John 1:3, Colossians 1:16).

- **The Second Angel's Message:**
  - Declare the fall of Babylon (Revelation 14:8): false systems of worship crumble under the truth of Jesus Christ.
  - Jesus, the Truth (John 14:6), calls His people out of spiritual confusion.
- **The Third Angel's Message:**
  - Warn of the consequences of rejecting Christ (Revelation 14:9-11).
  - Uplift Jesus' sacrificial death and resurrection as the only way to eternal life (John 3:16, Acts 4:12).
- **Transition:**
  "These messages are not merely warnings—they are an invitation to experience Jesus' victory over sin and eternal life."

4. Main Point

Key Phrase: *"The Three Angels' Messages are a call to worship Jesus, the Creator, Redeemer, and soon-coming King."*
Repeat this phrase throughout the sermon to reinforce the central focus on Christ.

5. Gospel Connection - God's Grace in Action:

- God sent Jesus to redeem humanity, demonstrating His love (Ephesians 2:8-9).
- Jesus' life, death, and resurrection fulfill the hope of the gospel (John 3:16).
- **The Holy Spirit's Role:**
  - The Spirit empowers us to live in alignment with God's truth (John 15:4-5).

- Through Christ, we can be victorious over sin and participate in His eternal kingdom (Romans 8:9-11).

6. Application - The Great Controversy in Real Time:

Apply the warnings of Revelation 14 to present-day distractions, deceptions, and the need for authentic worship.

- **Call for Commitment**:
  Encourage the audience to align their lives with the truth of the gospel and the Creator's call.
- **Transforming Power of Christ**:
  Jesus offers victory over sin and the hope of eternal life (Philippians 2:5-11). Through the Holy Spirit, believers are renewed and empowered to reflect God's character (2 Corinthians 5:17).

7. Appeal: Call for Transformation in Jesus

- **Conclude with One Key Statement**:
  "Jesus is the heart of the Three Angels' Messages—He calls us to worship Him, walk in His truth, and prepare for His glorious return."
- **Invitation**:
  Urge the audience to respond to Jesus today:
    - Surrender to His lordship.
    - Accept His redeeming grace.
    - Commit to worshiping Him as Creator, Redeemer, and soon-coming King.

Appeal Song: Choose a song like *"Jesus Paid It All"* or *"I Surrender All"* to reinforce the message.

Close with Prayer: Ask for the Holy Spirit's transforming power in the lives of all who hear.

End with the Blessing:
"May the everlasting gospel bring you peace, hope, and the assurance of salvation in Jesus Christ."

Appendix 2

Preaching the Three Angels Messages

Text: John 12:32 - "And I, if I be lifted up from the earth, will draw all men unto me."
Theme: Uplifting Jesus Christ

1. Introduction - Grab Attention: Start with an impactful statement or story that captures the heart of the Gospel.

- Transition to the Text: Introduce the biblical passage with a sense of expectation that this message will point to Jesus.
- Read the Text with Passion: Declare the words of John 12:32, with emphasis on the drawing power of Jesus' sacrifice.

2. Problem - Identify the Biblical Problem:

- Humanity's sin and disobedience (Romans 3:23; Titus 1:15).
- The reality of the Great Controversy between Christ and Satan (1 Peter 5:8; Revelation 12:4-9).
- Connect the Problem to the Text: Humanity is lost and in need of a Savior. The battle between Christ and Satan rages, with sin separating us from God.

3. Solution - The solution is found in Jesus Christ.

- Jesus' life, death, and resurrection offer salvation and victory over sin.
  - Uplift Jesus as the Savior who draws us to Himself (John 3:16; Acts 4:12).
- Connect to Victory in Jesus: His sacrifice on the cross provides redemption and reconciliation (John 12:32).

4. Main Point - Craft a Memorable Phrase:

- Example: "Lift Jesus up, and He will draw you to Himself."
- Make this key phrase central, repeating it throughout the sermon to reinforce the message.

5. Gospel Connection - Transition to the Good News:

    - Jesus, in His grace, offers redemption and transformation to all who believe (Romans 1:16).
    - God's Action: God's grace and mercy through Jesus' life, death, and resurrection (Ephesians 2:8-9; John 3:16).
    - Holy Spirit's Work: Through the Spirit, God transforms us (John 15:4-5; Colossians 1:24-29).

6. Application - Bridge from Biblical Times to Today:

    - We live in the reality of the Great Controversy, but the hope of Christ's victory is now.
    - Apply the main point: Lift up Jesus in our lives, and He will draw us closer to Him.
    - Life Transformation in Jesus: Speak of how Christ empowers us through the Holy Spirit for transformation (2 Corinthians 5:17; Romans 12:1-2).
    - Encourage the audience to allow the Holy Spirit to renew their hearts (Ephesians 4:22-24).

7. Appeal - Call to Transformation in Jesus:

    - Urge the congregation to lift up Jesus in their lives and invite Him to draw them closer.
    - Offer a personal invitation to accept Jesus as Savior today, knowing He desires to transform their lives.

Appendix 3

Preaching Text Study Questions

The "Finding Christ in the Text" Template:

- **Passage:**
- **Context:** (Historical, literary, theological)
- **Where is Christ in this passage?** (Foreshadowing, typology, direct reference)
- **Christ's Character Revealed:**

- How does this passage point to the Gospel?
- Application to Today:
- Challenge or Call to Action:

The Gospel Connection Template:

- Old Testament Text:
- How does this passage point to Christ?
- New Testament Fulfillment or Reflection:
- How does this shape the listener's understanding of Christ?
- How does it inspire transformation and growth?

The "4P Christ-Centered Outline" Template:

- **Passage:** Identify the Biblical text.
- **Picture of Christ:** Where do you see Christ's character, actions, or presence?
- **Purpose:** What is the main theological or Gospel-centered truth?
- **Practical Application:** How does this truth impact the lives of listeners?

"Text to Transformation" Flow Template:

- Scripture Reading:
- **Big Idea:** State the main Christ-centered message in one sentence.
- Breakdown:
  - Where is Jesus in the passage?

- **What does this reveal about His work (life, death, resurrection)?**
- **How does it meet our needs (grace, salvation, transformation)?**
- **Life Application:** What does this truth call us to be, believe, or do?
- **Call for Life Transformation in Jesus**

Bibliography

Adams, Jay E. *Preaching with Purpose: A Comprehensive Textbook on Biblical Preaching.* Grand Rapids: Zondervan, 1982.

Barrett, C. K. *The Gospel of St. John.* Philadelphia: Westminster Press, 1978.

Borchert, Gerald L. *Preaching the Word of God: The Evangelical Preacher's Guide to the Bible.* Grand Rapids: Baker Books, 2002.

Chappell, Bryan. *Christ-Centered Preaching: Redeeming the Expository Sermon.* Grand Rapids: Baker Books, 2005.

Chapell, Bryan. *The Gospel: How the Church Portrays the Beauty of Christ.* Wheaton, IL: Crossway, 2007.

Clowney, Edmund P. *Preaching Christ in All of Scripture.* Wheaton, IL: Crossway, 2003.

Collins, C. John. *Genesis 1-4: A Linguistic, Literary, and Theological Commentary.* Phillipsburg, NJ: P&R Publishing, 2006.

Dever, Mark. *Preaching: A Biblical Theology.* Nashville: B&H Academic, 2012.

Feinberg, John S. *The Many Faces of Evil: Theological Systems and the Problem of Evil.* Wheaton, IL: Crossway, 2004.

Gilbert, Greg. *What Is the Gospel?* Wheaton, IL: Crossway, 2010.

Harris, R. L. *Theological Wordbook of the Old Testament.* Chicago: Moody Press, 1980.

Heath, Matthew, and Michael Lawrence. *Preaching the Bible: The Art and Craft of Biblical Preaching.* Wheaton, IL: Crossway, 2017.

Hughes, R. Kent. *Liberating Exposition: New Perspectives on Biblical Preaching.* Grand Rapids: Baker Books, 2000.

Jenson, Robert W. *The Triune God.* Oxford: Oxford University Press, 2004.

Keller, Timothy. *Preaching: Communicating Faith in an Age of Skepticism.* New York: Viking, 2015.

Lloyd-Jones, D. Martyn. *Preaching and Preachers.* Grand Rapids: Zondervan, 1971.

Long, Thomas G. *The Witness of Preaching.* Louisville: Westminster John Knox Press, 2005.

MacArthur, John. *The Master's Plan for the Church.* Chicago: Moody Press, 1991.

Murray, Iain H. *The Puritan Hope: A Study in Revival and the Interpretation of Prophecy.* Edinburgh: Banner of Truth Trust, 1994.

Packer, J. I. *Knowing God.* Downers Grove, IL: InterVarsity Press, 1973.

Piper, John. *The Supremacy of God in Preaching.* Grand Rapids: Baker Books, 1990.

Stott, John. *Between Two Worlds: The Art of Preaching in the Twentieth Century.* Grand Rapids: Eerdmans, 1982.

Tennent, Timothy C. *The Great Commission: Evangelicals and the History of World Missions.* Grand Rapids: Baker Academic, 2010.

Tripp, Paul David. *Dangerous Calling: Confronting the Unique Challenges of Pastoral Ministry.* Wheaton, IL: Crossway, 2012.

Vickers, Brian. *Christ-Centered Preaching: Reaching the Heart with the Gospel.* Wheaton, IL: Crossway, 2011.

Wright, N. T. *How God Became King: The Forgotten Story of the Gospels.* New York: HarperOne, 2012.

Wright, N. T. *Simply Jesus: A New Vision of Who He Was, What He Did, and Why He Matters.* New York: HarperOne, 2011.

Zuck, Roy B. *Basic Bible Interpretation: A Practical Guide to Discovering Biblical Meaning.* Nashville: Victor Books, 1991.

Robinson, Haddon W. *Biblical Preaching: The Development and Delivery of Expository Messages.* Grand Rapids: Baker Academic, 2001.

Robinson, Haddon W., and Scott M. Gibson. *Making a Difference in Preaching: A Guide for Communication.* Grand Rapids: Baker Academic, 2012.

Stuart, Douglas K. *Old Testament Exegesis: A Handbook for Students and Pastors.* Louisville: Westminster John Knox Press, 2001.

Bauckham, Richard. *The Theology of the Book of Revelation.* Cambridge: Cambridge University Press, 1993.

Vines, Jerry. *The Anatomy of a Preaching Ministry: A Handbook for Developing Your Preaching Ministry.* Nashville: Thomas Nelson, 1993.

McGrath, Alister. *The Christian Theology Reader.* Oxford: Blackwell Publishing, 2006.

Sears, Charles. *Effective Bible Preaching: How to Communicate God's Word to the Modern Listener.* Grand Rapids: Zondervan, 2001.

Hunter, James Davison. *To Change the World: The Irony, Tragedy, and Possibility of Christianity in the Late Modern World.* New York: Oxford University Press, 2010.

Migliore, Daniel L. *Faith Seeking Understanding: An Introduction to Christian Theology.* Grand Rapids: Eerdmans, 2004.

Hendriksen, William. *Exposition of the Gospel According to Matthew.* Grand Rapids: Baker Book House, 1973.

Wright, Christopher J. H. *The Mission of God's People: A Biblical Theology of the Church's Mission.* Grand Rapids: Zondervan, 2010.

Anderson, Greg. *The Power of God in Preaching: A Comprehensive Guide for Preaching.* Wheaton, IL: Crossway, 2009.

Towns, Elmer L. *Preaching to the Church: A How-To Guide for Preachers and Teachers.* Nashville: Thomas Nelson, 1997.

Owen, John. *The Death of Death in the Death of Christ.* Edinburgh: Banner of Truth Trust, 2004.

Green, Michael. *Evangelism in the Early Church.* Grand Rapids: Eerdmans, 2004.

Burge, Gary M. *John: The NIV Application Commentary.* Grand Rapids: Zondervan, 2000.

Kistemaker, Simon J. *Exposition of the Epistle to the Hebrews.* Grand Rapids: Baker Book House, 1984.

Morris, Leon. *The Apostolic Preaching of the Cross.* Grand Rapids: Eerdmans, 1982.

Naylor, Michael. *Preaching: A Guide for the Faithful.* London: SPCK, 1997.

Kuyper, Abraham. *The Work of the Holy Spirit.* Grand Rapids: Baker Books, 2004.

Gibson, Scott M. *Preaching for the Glory of God: A Theology of the Pulpit.* Grand Rapids: Baker Books, 2005.

Lewis, C. S. *The Great Divorce.* San Francisco: HarperOne, 2001.

Subscribe to

Youtube.com/AdventPreaching

Notes

Made in the USA
Middletown, DE
31 December 2024